How to Become a Successful Author While Working Full-Time: The Secret to Work-Life Balance

Ron Vitale

ISBN: 1544885237
ISBN–13: 9781544885230

Visit Ron Vitale's website at www.RonVitale.com

Mom,

Thank you for everything you've done for me.

Love,

Ron

Also by Ron Vitale

Lost: Cinderella's Secret Witch Diaries (Book 1)

Stolen: Cinderella's Secret Witch Diaries (Book 2)

Found: Cinderella's Secret Witch Diaries (Book 3)

Faith: The Jovian Gate Chronicles (Book 1)

The Jovian Gate Chronicles: Short Story Collection

Awakenings: A Witch's Coven (Book 1)

Betrayals: A Witch's Coven (Book 2)

Dorothea's Song

Chapter 1 Starting Out

Congratulations on taking a step to help advance your writing career. No matter if this is your first book or your tenth, I am here to help. I started indie publishing back in 2008, and it's been a long and strange trip since then. The publishing industry was, and is, in flux, and the story I will tell, along with the skills I learned that I'll share with you, will help you become a more successful writer.

But first, I expect you'll want to know a little about me. I am the director of Web Technology at a large public university on the East Coast. I manage a team of three and am integrated with a larger team on enhancing the web enterprise at the university, focusing on a user-first approach. I am extremely busy with my full-time day job. Sometimes I am up in the middle of the night when websites are down, and there are often emails to be answered in the "off hours" or on the weekend. I love my full-time job, and yet, I had dreamed of being a writer ever since I was nine years old. I watched old-school *Doctor Who* back in the '80s, fell in love with *Star Wars*, read *The Fellowship of the Ring,* and played *Dungeons & Dragons*, hoping that one day I would grow up to be a "novelist."

Back in elementary school (we called it "grade" school when I was growing up), I wrote stories in my Pac-Man notebook, drew pictures of the aliens I created, and started to formulate ideas that became stories. In my early teen years, my stories evolved into *Dungeons & Dragons* role-playing adventures that I tried to get published in *Dragon* magazine. I purchased a Smith Corona electric typewriter (that came with changeable keys for foreign characters when I wrote up my French papers for school). I started to submit my role-playing adventures and stories to various publications, but I kept failing time and time again.

At age sixteen, I wrote my first novel, and over the course of twenty years, I submitted it to more publishing houses and literary agents than I can remember. It was rejected up and down the block. I followed the rules of no simultaneous submissions to publishing houses and dealt with the frustration of never hearing back from places (even after I followed to the letter the instructions in providing a SASE [self-addressed stamped envelope]). If it were not for the digital revolution and Amazon disrupting the publishing world with Kindle Direct Publishing (KDP), I expect my story would end there. I would have kept trying to submit my book to traditional publishers and eventually given up.

In the last eight years, my output exploded exponentially with my publishing not only the first three books of the *Cinderella's Secret Witch Diaries* series but also two books in *A Witch's Coven* series, my first novel in *The Realms* series, and book one in *The Jovian Gate Chronicles*. To date, I've published seven novels, a short story collection, and a book on nonfiction. I took my dream and found a way to make it become reality—all while working a full-time job and raising a family.

I expect your writing journey is different than mine, but there is one thing that we have in common: We all started out somewhere and needed to make a decision to write more. No matter if you started with a short story, poem (I went through my sensitive poetry phase in the '90s), or novels, our desire to write stayed with us. If you do not have that drive, then this book is not for you.

What I am going to share is a story of failure mixed with success. I work full-time and spend (with commuting time included) eleven hours each day on my job. The remaining time I have, I need to carve up for my kids, wife, sleep, eating, exercise, chores, recreation, and you got it, writing.

Working full-time at a job and being an author who writes full-length novels is not easy. I expect you know that or you wouldn't have purchased this book. I'm a firm believer of admitting and voicing what I struggle against. Before we start, I want you to say this with me: Writing books is hard. Damn hard.

Feels good to say it, but it might feel a bit stupid, too.

One of the lessons I've learned since I started this journey is that what I do is not easily understood by my friends or family. Many people think I just sit down, write, everything magically just gets done, and a book goes up on sale. When people ask me about "how do I do it all," I can tell the moment when they've lost interest. People don't really want to know how the sausage is made. They just want the quick five-second answer.

But you've made a decision to advance your career. And that's a good thing. You've taken the first step to admit you need help. Something isn't working for you. No matter if it's the logistical aspects of writing, juggling various hats, or work-life balance, you're here for a reason. The good news is I'm here for you. We're going on this crazy writing journey together. And together, we'll get there.

You're Not Alone

A writer's life is often solitary and can be lonely. We do research, read, and then sit down and write. But if you've not yet reached out to fellow writers, I am here to help. When I started out, I had questions upon questions, and several people in the indie publishing world helped me find the answers I needed.

You can do the same. Join a forum discussion on Kindleboards.com, a Facebook group, or listen to podcasts and then join in the conversation. For many long years, I tried networking in the wrong places. Back in college, I tried asking my professors for help, but they couldn't help me because they weren't published fiction authors. They wrote scholarly papers for literary critique magazines and had no background on the publishing industry. As the industry changed and indie publishing rose to prominence, I tried to learn as much as I could. But here's the secret I've figured out over time: writing and all that surrounds it (more on that in a moment) is like trying to drink from a fire hose. If you dive all in, you'll get blasted by a powerful stream of cold water that will knock you senseless.

There have been times in which I have been overwhelmed and felt lost on where to go, who to talk to, what to do next, and how to achieve my goals. For me, what I found extremely helpful over time is to look at writing as a journey that never ends. If I am traveling the world, there will be times in which I need to work to pay for my travels. I need to research to learn about the places I'm headed and then need to drive, fly, or walk to the next destination. I cannot simply just go to all the places at once or have the money to even do that. I need a plan, people to talk to for advice, and a quiet time to process and make important decisions.

Here are some practical ways to learn about writing, the business of writing, and marketing:

Podcasts

- *The Art of Paid Traffic with Rick Mulready*
- *The Author Biz*
- *The Creative Penn podcast*

- *Kobo Writing Life podcast*
- *The Rocking Self-Publishing podcast*
- The Self-Publishing Podcast Classics
- *The Smart Passive Income podcast*
- *Story Grid podcast*
- *The Tim Ferriss Show*
- *Unemployable with Brian Clark*

Blogs

- *Writer Beware*
- *Kristine Kathryn Rusch's Business Musing*
- *Kindleboards*
- *Creative Penn*

What I've listed here is only a short list of resources, but even if you try to listen or read everything, you'll quickly realize you'll have no time to write. When I first started writing, I quickly became overwhelmed. I went from feeling lonely to being overloaded with information overnight. What will work for you? I don't know. I can only share with you that I slowly added podcasts to my weekly routine. I'll try a new podcast out, listen to an episode or two, and move on if I don't think it's a good fit for me. Or, I might listen to a particular episode if the topic is on something that I want to learn.

The same thing is true of blogs. There are many other blogs where I go to read and learn about writing, but I tend to dip in on a more regular basis to the ones listed above. If you're looking to learn and connect with like-minded people, the few resources I listed above can get you started. From there, you'll hear about other writers who are being interviewed, and you can then branch out and follow them.

I make time to listen to the podcasts on my morning and evening commutes. On the weekends, when I'm doing chores, I turn on a podcast while cleaning the bathroom, and it's a great way to listen, learn, and clean. I love it! There are more writing communities online than either of us have time to participate in. Explore and slowly add to your weekly routine. Over time, you'll take in what you've learned and start making connections on how to apply your newfound knowledge with the practical everyday tasks ahead of you.

Chapter 2: Defining Your Goal

What does the term "successful writer" mean to you? Do you want to finish your first book, produce a trilogy, or sell millions of copies around the world and become the next J. K. Rowling? The definition of success can be personal, financial, tied to fame, or a mix of all three.

When I first started out, I had only one goal in mind: I wanted to finish *Lost: Cinderella's Secret Witch Diaries* to dedicate the book to my daughter. But a funny thing happened along the way. All those years of dreaming of being a writer suddenly rushed back, and I realized that I didn't just want to write one book, but I wanted to write a trilogy. Back when I was sixteen years old, I wrote my first book and thought that the well had gone dry. Many years later, I wrote a sequel to *Dorothea's Song* but never published it. I had created a fantasy world and thought I hit my creative peak young and would never be able to come up with another set of characters, let alone a new world.

I wrote some stories along the way, but I never tried to write another book outside the fantasy world of *The Realms* that I had created. I didn't think I had the creative spark within me to write other books. I had no goals outside of: I want to publish a book.

I languished along in my twenties and thirties, and then something happened to me. When I turned thirty-eight years old, I was hit by my mid-life crisis. I looked back and saw all the hard work I had done for my day job and in spending time with my family, but I had not invested in myself. I had not set goals for myself around the dream of "I want to be a writer." I had no clue on what to do, where to go, how to start, or even if I could do it. I felt like a failure and overwhelmed. My dream of writing and publishing a book seemed an impossibility.

And then the perfect storm hit: I met new colleagues at work who inspired me to break out of the mold I had set myself, and a spark of an idea came to me. Instead of tossing the idea away, I jotted it down and then took a leap of faith and decided I wanted to write a book. One day I was going about my merry way, and the next I was a writer. The switch, for me, happened instantaneously. One night when

I was putting my daughter to bed, I was reading her *Cinderella*. I finished, tucked my daughter into bed, and an idea struck me:

What happened to Cinderella after she married the prince?

I didn't look for the idea—I hadn't been thinking about getting back into writing—I just allowed my mind to be open and be creative. Shortly after I had the idea, I discovered it wasn't going to go away. I had written it down and needed to make a decision: Let it go or write the damn book.

I chose to write the book. I defined my goal and simply said: "I'm going to do this." But the next step was critical for me. I started telling my friends and family I was going to write a book. I defined my goal for myself and then spoke my commitment to the world and knew that I was serious this time. I needed to hold true to my word.

My daughter was almost three at the time, my son almost seven, and I had an extremely challenging full-time job. When the hell was I going to have time to write a novel? I had no clue. The last time I had written a book I was sixteen years old and had plenty of time after school. Now I was a father with a demanding job. How?

It took me eighteen months to write the book because I had no idea how to do it. At one point, I stopped writing because I felt burned out and then needed to slowly force myself into the swing of things. But the big secret that I learned about how to actually make the time to write was simpler than I had expected. As corny as it might sound, I took the Nike motto to heart: "Just do it."

After I told my friends and family I was writing a book, I tried an experiment. I took my personal laptop to work for a few days, and over lunch (which I began taking instead of working at my desk), I closed my office door, fired up my laptop, and started writing. After I did that for a bit, I came up with another plan. I started getting up early and wrote before work. I carved time out in the morning between 5:30 a.m. and 6:30 a.m. on an irregular basis.

Over time, five hundred words become twelve hundred, and about a year in, I had the first draft of my book.

From a practical standpoint, defining my goal helped me firm up my commitment, and then I could get started. My goal has since evolved because I have completed my goal. To date, I have published seven novels and one collection of short stories. My goal now is to continue writing books but to focus on broadening my reader base and achieving more financial success.

What is your goal? How are you going to achieve it? When are you going to start?

The best tip I'll share is to make room in your life for writing. I cut back on TV, sleep, and entertainment (going to the movies, playing games, etc.). I made room in my life for writing, and I held myself accountable to that by telling people I loved. When I would meet up with friends, they'd ask me "How is the book writing going?" Some cared, some didn't, but having spoken the words of my goal, and then making space in my life to achieve it, set off a revolution for me that years later I'm still at it, and I am working full-time at my day job. It is possible to do both if you have a plan.

The Hare Versus the Tortoise

Are you a hare or a tortoise? When I was a kid, one of my nicknames was "rabbit" because I was fast and had buckteeth. I used to flit about working really hard and succeeded because I could put my mind to a task, finish it quickly, and move on to the next goal.

When I applied this technique to writing *Lost*, I couldn't figure out how to navigate through all the work. I had a goal clearly defined: I wanted to write a book about what happened to Cinderella after she married the prince. But that's about all I had. Well, I did have the responsibilities of the full-time job, travel for work, long hours, and a whole host of other pressing tasks that pulled me away from writing.

I'd work really hard, come home, and just want to veg. I would be out of the house from 7:30 a.m. and wouldn't get home until 6:30 p.m. There would be dinner, cleaning up, and then putting the kids to bed (or as my wife and I used to joke: "bed, bath, and beyond…").

No matter how fast I was, I couldn't reconcile the fact that I couldn't write a book in one or two weeks. I tried writing faster but hit a wall called burnout (more on that fun topic in a later chapter).

I quickly discovered that no matter how fast I tried to go, I needed to find a system that would be sustaining for the long haul. I couldn't just try to knock out a book because I had to learn not just the writing craft but also marketing and the business aspect of a writing career—all while working my day job and raising a family.

How did I fix my problem? I changed my perspective. Instead of trying to write monster lengths of the book at thousands of words at a time, I pulled back and slowed down. The tricky thing is that instead of writing in bursts when my "muse" spoke to me, I kept writing on a more regular basis. The race to the finish line wasn't simply a hundred-yard dash. I envisioned it as a marathon, and it's probably no coincidence that I began training for my first marathon while writing book number two in the *Cinderella's Secret Witch Diaries* series.

Slow and steady worked extremely well for me. But no matter if I were writing or training for the marathon, there was a little voice inside my head that would taunt me, forcing me to compare myself with others.

Compare Is to Deflate

After I finished my first book in eighteen months, I patted myself on the back and basked in my success. But then I started talking with other writers and learned that other authors were writing as many as fifteen books a year. The same thing happened when I completed my first marathon. I finished the 26.2-mile race in five hours and six minutes. My friends ran a lot faster, and I learned that years back Oprah had finished her marathon in less than five hours. The accomplishment of finishing a book and a marathon should have been happy and amazing achievements for me, but instead I focused on comparing my results to others.

What that did was simple: I devalued my own success, and that deflated my self-esteem.

Over time, I came to the conclusion that it's not helpful to compare myself to others. I am not Oprah or writing fifteen books a year. Who I am is a multifaceted person, and my achievements can only be compared to my own life. In running, the term "PR" stands for personal record. When I completed my first marathon, I had achieved a personal record. I had gone from never having run a marathon to completing one in five hours and six minutes. Considering I never thought I would ever run a marathon in my life, I achieved an amazing feat.

Over the years, I have taken the PR concept and applied it to writing. When I hear of other writers who have had great success, I do not try to compare myself to them but congratulate them on their hard work and then focus on what I can control in my writing life. I now compare myself to my own work and experiences.

Writing, like running, is a mental game. Fatigue, doubt, and fear all creep up to pull you down. When people ask me how I ran a marathon, I tell them about the training. You don't just start out running twenty-six miles. No, instead you start out running one mile, then a few, and over years, you build up the muscles to run four miles several times a week and do a long run on the weekends. Then each week after that, you tack on an additional mile so that slowly, over time, you reach your goal.

I try hard not to compare myself to others and focus on being the tortoise. I hope to have decades left in my writing career, and if I train and plan well, I'll be much more successful rather than burning out like the hare.

Chapter 3: Creating a Schedule

Each day, like clockwork, I get up for work. I have to be at my desk by 8:30 a.m. and know that I need to shower, dress, eat breakfast, and rush to the train. I do not have these steps written down because they've become second nature to me over the last twenty years. I know where I need to be, by when, and just get there on time.

But writing was always different for me. I would listen to my muse sing to me, and I'd hope the inspiration would cause me to become creative and then I'd write. I had this down to a science. I would get an idea, and if I didn't start on it within a day or two, I'd lose the inspiration, and it would fade away forever. Over time, I'd make the effort to write and over a week or two a cool short story would come out of my hard work.

I never truly grasped the difference between waiting to be inspired and writing as a job. For my entire life, writing was always built up as this magical thing. I'd get an idea, chase after the fairy dust, and I'd somehow find a way to take the idea and capture it in words. Sounds pretty, doesn't it?

Writing 7,500 words for a short story and around 70,000 (or more) words for a novel is entirely different. When I started out on *Lost*, I knew the basic premise of the story, but I didn't know any of the characters outside of Cinderella and the prince. I just knew that I had a general idea, and so I started writing. Yet a funny thing happened to me a few weeks in on the project: I hit a wall. I didn't know what to do next in the story. Where was my magical muse that would whisper in my ear and I'd translate that beautiful vision into the frail words that we humans use daily?

I look back and have to laugh at myself. Not to make fun of my situation, but a transformation has taken place in my writing habits. I learned that just like I need to go to work on a regular basis to complete the projects I'm part of there, that I also need a regular schedule for writing. I needed to start showing up. I had heard fellow writers talk about "butt in chair," but I didn't really understand what that meant. I just wrote when I felt like it and wasn't really getting anywhere.

Now I've talked with other writers about a schedule, and the "S" word can be scary for some. Do I have a whole spreadsheet created that I can share with you and you'll have direct insight into my writing process? No. It's not because I don't want to share with you my personal schedule, but there is no spreadsheet. I have an extremely simple schedule.

I go to my full-time job Monday through Friday with the weekends off. Here is my schedule:

Sunday morning: Long run
Monday morning: Writing
Tuesday morning: Four-mile run
Wednesday morning: Writing
Thursday morning: Four-mile run
Friday morning: Writing
Saturday morning: Writing

Let me break this down for you and go through my schedule with you.

Monday

I get up around 5:00 a.m. to 5:30 a.m. (I don't use an alarm clock and just let my body get up naturally.) I go downstairs, fire up the laptop, and write for about forty-five minutes to one hour.

I then eat breakfast, rush upstairs for a shower, and take my son to school by 7:00 a.m. If I get to work early, I log into Google Drive and finish writing if I woke up "late" or was in the middle of a scene. By 8:30 a.m., I start my day job and log out of Google Drive.

Tuesday

I get up around 5:00 a.m. to 5:30 a.m. and go run four miles. This takes me around forty0 minutes. I then factor in time to stretch, eat breakfast, and then rush off to work.

Wednesday

It's a repeat of Monday. The only difference is that I don't have to get my son to school by 7:00 a.m., so I can take it easy and not rush so much.

Thursday

Thursday is a repeat of Tuesday.

Friday

Friday is a repeat of Monday.

Saturday

I get up the same time as normal (unless I sleep in until 6:00 a.m.) and go downstairs to write. The kids and my wife tend to sleep in, so I can normally get an hour or two in before anyone else gets up. After chores, I might sneak in some writing in the afternoon or work on marketing, social media, etc. All depends on what we're doing with the kids that day.

Sunday

I'm usually running by 6:00 a.m. I like to run anywhere between eight and thirteen miles, depending on whether I'm training for a race. When I'm training for a marathon (I've only done three so it's pretty rare), my runs could go as long as four hours. I'll talk more about that in the burnout chapter, but I found that for my sanity and my family's, it's easier if I stick to half-marathon races.

The schedule I created for myself is easy to follow and has lots of flexibility in it. If I'm not able to write for whatever reason, I can get the work done during lunch or at night. I learned that it's helpful to have such flexibility because I might need to stay late at work or come in early for a meeting.

By having a regular schedule, I learned two things:

1.   Even 1,000 words per writing day quickly adds up.
     i.   One week of writing (Monday, Wednesday, Friday, and Saturday) = 4,000 words

        ii.   4,000 words * 16 weeks (4 months) = 64,000 words

   2.   Even writing at a slow pace, over a couple of months, I can write the first draft of a novel. Interesting, isn't it?

Add another couple of months of time for rewriting and you have a book in a year. Now you could decide to go faster or slower, but I gave a basic example so that you would have a sense of how small amounts of writing over time can add up to a completed book.

But there's the elephant in the room that I need to address…

How to Become a Disciplined Writer

When I first started this schedule, I sat down on Monday morning and knocked out my 1,000-word goal. Woo-hoo! Completed. I then had off on Tuesday to run. Wednesday morning I sat back down and still had some gas in the tank, Thursday I ran, but on Friday and Saturday, I hit inspiration walls.

I don't believe in writer's block. I know that might not be popular to say, but I just don't. I believe in fear, not wanting to work on a project, but I don't believe in being "blocked."

The writing schedule I created for myself was designed to help me break through those walls when I didn't have any ideas. Through the rest of the week, I used the limited free time I had to read, listen to podcasts, watch movies or TV, talk to people, and pursue other sorts of creative outlets. I was taking in lots of information but needed to find a way to recharge my batteries and also let my mind wander.

I never had a true grasp on how I became inspired and when my muse spoke to me until I started this schedule. When I just wrote throughout the week, I was missing the other side of the coin, and I'd get creative ideas while driving or in the shower. As soon as I added the running to my weekly schedule, I realized I had found the perfect match. By building in quiet time while running, I had hours of "me time" set up to help my brain just be and work out whatever it waned while I exercised.

When I run, I suit up and go run. I do not listen to music because it's a distraction for me. I've had people question how I can run without music, and what I do is to simply let my mind wander. Maybe I start working out a problem in my life. Or I might think of my plans for the next few days, but often, out of the blue, ideas about the book I'm working on come to me.

The big secret is that my most creative time comes from running, gardening, and cleaning bathrooms (I kid you not.). There's something about working with my body and not actively trying to "be creative" that really works for me. Now that most of us have smartphones, no matter where I'm at, I can take a simple note down.

Yes, there are still times in which I don't quite have a plot figured out, and I've made some mistakes over the years, but I've become better at allowing myself the time to daydream and be inspired. When I wrote the third book in my *Cinderella's Secret Witch Diaries* series, I finished the first draft and came to the conclusion that a third of the book just didn't work. When I read the draft, it depressed even me, and I wrote it! So I tossed it and went back to work. Sitting down and looking at the blank page can be frightening, but I've changed the conversation in my head on that.

Instead I look at the white page as a blank canvas, and I can write whatever I want on it. I just let myself go. My best times writing come when I see a scene in my head, like there's a movie playing, and I simply start typing away, desperately trying to capture in words what I'm envisioning. But I needed to carve out time in my weekly schedule to allow myself the creative freedom to consciously (or subconsciously) work on the plot problems in my books.

My first drafts range from sucking really bad to having some solid scenes in them. But it doesn't matter, because at the end of the day, I have words to work with and reshape. Now when I sit down to write, I have an idea in mind. What are the characters up to? Where is the tension or suspense? I write those scenes out, linking them together to tell the narrative.

The trick that I use is that I'll write a scene and end in the middle of something exciting happening so that I can pick up the threads of the plot to continue where I left off when I next sit down to write.

Do I need to become better at this? Certainly. I hope to keep learning and becoming a better writer because that's important to me. I want to become better at my craft. But without discipline and sticking to my schedule, I was constantly trying to chase after my goal of completing a novel because I was being ineffective. Now, my schedule allows for room to write as well as daydreaming to work the plot out.

Be Accountable

Before I go any further, I want to share a story. It's easy for me to write a few words down and talk about the magic plan to work full-time and how I've written book after book. The words that I've written here only tell part of the story, and I want to get real.

If you are at a point in which you have decided to write a book, then you have many choices. You can do the work or you cannot. I think of Yoda at this time.

"Do or do not, there is no try."

When you are faced with getting up early or staying up late, you will need to make a decision. Either you are going to do the work or you're not. Here is where I would ask that you be honest with yourself. Writing is not easy. Learning marketing is not easy. Nor is understanding how to run a business. You will need to do all of these things (and more) if you choose to be an indie author.

If the amount of work in front of you is scary and you'd rather not do it, then do yourself a favor and don't. That might sound harsh, but there truly isn't a "try." Writing 40,000 words and giving up, sure you can do that, but why waste the time?

I would recommend that you look yourself in a mirror and be honest with yourself. Either make the commitment to do the work or don't. Dragging the work out for years or decades isn't going to help you. There is no shame in making a decision that you do not want to be a writer. One's identity isn't tied into what we do.

Being creative can come out in all forms and trades and does not need to be tied to writing a book. Draw, teach, sing, dance, or just write short stories for fun. But if you're serious about being an indie author who writes novels, the next step I would highly recommend is a big one.

Be accountable.

What does that really mean?

I'll show you. Here is my Google Sheets word count document (smarturl.it/ronswriting) that is a breakdown of my weekly writing goals during the time I wrote *Betrayals*. I started writing the book on February 25, 2015. I believe being accountable means that I set a goal, share what the goal is to my family and friends, and then meet that goal.

Does that mean that the world should stop and you sacrifice everything to meet your writing goal? No.

There are times when your kids are sick, you need to stay late at work, or some other unexpected event comes up. You might be hitting the burnout wall and decide to take a day off. That's okay. Forward momentum is important, and if you look at my tracking sheet, you'll see not only how much work I did over the various months it took me to write the book, but you'll also see that in March I was working on other things (I needed to review the nearly nine hours of audio files for *Lost* as I was working with a voice actor to have the book published on Audible.).

From my tracking, you can see that I started the book in late February through March and then took a break in April and May since I was working to publish *Awakenings* (Book 1 in the *Witch's Coven* series). Once *Awakenings* was published, I switched back, and then during July through August, I finished the book, releasing *Betrayals* in September 2015.

I held myself accountable because I believe it's critical to make a goal and strive to achieve it. I put my butt in the chair and wrote.

If I can do it, so can you. And the secret is that I gave myself permission to achieve my goal. I stopped thinking about the words, the tracking, but kept my plan really simple. I knew that on Mondays, Wednesdays, Fridays, and Saturdays I wrote. Tuesdays, Thursdays, and Sundays, I ran. On writing days, I'd get up, write and write the number of words down, close up my laptop, and go about my day.

When I ran, I'd use the time to dream, think, let go, relax, and to allow my body to just be. The yin-yang of it all made sense to me because although creating a schedule is important, it's the whole package of your life which gets you across the finish line.

Chapter 4: Commit to Yourself

Make the Commitment

So you've decided to write a book and be held accountable for meeting that goal. That's great news! But making a promise and living up to it is an entirely different thing. If you want to be a chef, you need to cook, bake, practice, and talk with other chefs in order to become better.

The same is true of writing. I've met many authors who want to write and talk about the book idea they have, but they never write a word. Or, they'll start, stop, and give up.

It's safe to tell people you are an author but then never take the risk. Taking a risk and possibly failing is hard. I don't like to fail, but the truth is that I've failed more times than I can remember. I like to tell people that when I fail, I take some time to lick my wounds, get up, dust off my knees, and get back into the saddle again. I wish there was an easier way to do it, but I don't know of any shortcuts and haven't heard any from other authors.

When I turned thirty-eight, I decided to commit to being an author (and all that entails in the twenty-first century). I continue to learn my craft, read up and study marketing trends, network with like-minded authors, and keep moving forward—no matter how slow it might seem sometimes.

The secret is to make a commitment to invest in yourself. That might sound odd, but we invest in the stock market, in how much we commit to our loved ones, our jobs, and all sorts of activities, but I've found that it's often hard to take time to invest in ourselves. Education is key. I have been lucky to have gone to college and also obtained my master's in English literature. The critical thinking, reading, and writing skills I learned in my college years have enabled me to lay a solid foundation from which to build.

I'm not saying you must have a college education to be a good writer, but I do believe having a curious mind and wanting to learn is essential. Taking ideas that pop into your head and translating those ephemeral ideas to words that then are printed into a book or made into an ebook is pretty amazing when you stop and think about it.

The challenge is that an author's journey is never ending. There is always something new to learn. The publishing world is changing by disruptors like Amazon, honing your craft (dialogue and character development for me) might take years, and the marketing world is exploding with opportunities (Facebook ads, pixel tracking, Bookbub, going wide with a release, sticking only with Amazon via KDP select, and even Instafreebie promotions).

There are times I feel overwhelmed. I wouldn't be surprised if you feel the same. Where does one begin? The good news is that if you're following along in this book, you're well on your way:

- Define your goal
- Create a schedule

And now simply commit to investing in yourself. I can hear a few of you now already yelling, "But there are only twenty-four hours in the day? How am I supposed to do all of this work? How am I supposed to know what is 'good' work to do and what is wasting my time?"

I've been there, and to be honest, I sometimes fall down, asking those same questions still when a new challenge arises. I'm human and I screw up, become overwhelmed, and lose faith and sometimes my way. But what I've found to be great help is committing to building a life that will support my goal of being an author.

The Mind

In the last chapter, I wrote about the mind. I think this is the part that everyone can grasp (though it's daunting). To write well, we need to read other writers to learn what works (and what doesn't), practice our craft, learn about it, and suck up as much knowledge as we possibly can through books, podcasts, blogs, networking, Facebook groups, forums, etc. There aren't enough hours in the day to learn everything. There is too much information. The information flow is so great that if we stick our head in, we'll get whacked, and it's going to hurt.

We cannot work all the time, and yes, part of the mind shift is that I have seen "work" turn into "play" because I've come to love writing. I've seen it less as a chore and more as a means of letting my thoughts stream out and having lots of fun. The same can be said about some books or podcasts that I listen to, but usually I need to be fully engaged because I'm learning a new skill, and that means it takes concentration, energy, and a commitment on my part to be open to learning.

The problem that I have is that there is a lack of time. I use my morning and afternoon commute from work (which is almost an hour each way) to read or listen to podcasts. But not always. Sometimes I'm so stressed out with work deadlines and other challenges going on in my life that I just want to listen to some music. I've worked hard on listening to what my body needs.

With using my mind, I've learned when I begin hitting the "I'm overloaded limit" by seeing how cranky I am to others and when my productivity goes down. Learning all there is to know about writing is great, but I also need to take a break. I can't always read, listen to podcasts, write, or work. It's just not possible. The biggest thing I learned after my burnout/meltdown of 2015 is this:

I cannot do it all.

And that's okay. When it comes to the mind, we have a lot of power over how we see ourselves and our place in the world, in our workplace, and our families. I do believe in the power of positivity. If we believe we're going to fail, then we will. Self-fulfilling prophecies come true all the time. I would much rather admit that I might fail, but I can then also pick myself up and keep on trying. The act of failing for me is a learning experience and enables me to grow in ways I couldn't foresee.

The Body

When I was younger, my metabolism was through the roof, and my family would joke with me about whether I had a secret compartment in my leg where I kept all the food that I ate. I would walk and bike from time to time, but I did nothing active outside of walking to the train, chores around the house, and light gardening work in the spring and summer. That's about it.

In my late thirties, I started noticing a middle-age paunch that started to form. I thought nothing of any of this, accepting the fact that I was getting older and needed to juggle work, family, and writing. About this time, friends of mine started running and gave my wife and

I a treadmill. My wife started using it, and several months in, I started to use the treadmill too. I didn't hate it, but I didn't necessarily like it. Our friends then challenged us to try a 5K run on New Year's Day, and we signed up, figuring that it would be fun to say we ran that far.

To train for the 5K, I ran around my kids' school and started out small. First it was three blocks, then four, and over time, I started adding a little more until I finally figured out how to breathe while running (They say that breathing is sort of important!), and I even subscribed to *Runner's World* magazine in order to read about this crazy new sport I had fallen into.

On the day of the race, my friends and I ran the 5K on a subfreezing New Year's Day on a boardwalk by the sea. We all had been up late the night before to celebrate the new year, and I remember how we finished the race, came back to our friends' house, and all collapsed on the sofas. We were amazed that we had done it. We all had completed a 5K race and survived! Those 3.1 miles flew by, and I remember how the cold air hurt my lungs as I breathed in, the sweat, and the great sense of accomplishment I felt when I crossed the finish line.

Months later our friends challenged us to run a ten-miler, and I agreed, then a half-marathon, and eventually a marathon. I see now what my friends were doing to me. They gradually kept raising the distance with talk such as: "Well, if you ran a 5K, you can do ten miles." The whole process took almost three years from my couch to completing a marathon.

Did I run a fast marathon? No, but I did make it in five hours and six minutes. I ran my first 5K in something like thirty-one minutes, and if you would have told me then that I would be able to run for more than five hours straight, I would have thought you were crazy. But I learned something about the human body: We are adaptable and can, over time, build up a tolerance to do amazing things.

It's not possible to just sit down and write a novel either; it takes practice, reading, trial and error over time. Writing a novel isn't impossible, but it helps to build up to writing a book after practicing. The same was true for me with exercising.

As luck would have it, my friends pulled me into running, and I tried it and liked it. I don't know what you might like. Some of my friends like cycling, walking, and even rowing a dragon boat. What works for you might be entirely different for me, and life circumstances will hit you, forcing you to adapt. Whatever you decide to do for exercise, please check in with your doctor and make certain it's safe for you to do.

Why do I run? I discovered that exercise allows me to let go of conscious thought and puts me into a flow state of mind. Running fuels my writing. I can just put on my sneakers and go. When I run, I have the freedom of the road stretching out before me, and the exercise unites my mind and body. It's a personal symbiotic relationship. I can strengthen my body and also work out a problem I'm having with the plot of a novel, become inspired with a new book, or even resolve character conflict by just running and letting my mind wander. When I run, I allow myself to daydream.

But I also found a deeper and more profound byproduct of running: self-esteem. When I started running, I chose not to listen to music because I liked having my mind wander, and it also gave me a chance to see the beauty of the world around me. A flower on the side of the road. A dog sticking his head out a passenger window as a car zoomed by or even the stars in the sky that lit up over me like the jewels of the Nile. I found connection between the world and me. Yet something happened to me after mile ten in training for the marathon. I realized I had to find a way to fight fatigue and doubt. There was a voice inside my head that would say "Stop. You're tired. You've done enough. You'll never be fast in running, just give up." The same voice has popped into my head about writing: "You suck. No one likes your work. Who do you think you are that you can write something of importance?"

My mind has played tricks on me all through my growing up and through adulthood. That voice in my head wanted me to fail because failure was safe. It was known. Failure would allow me to continue to hide away from the world instead of risking my voice and finding what I had always wanted: true joy in sharing what I created.

So what does the body have to do with any of this? I stumbled upon the connection between my mind and body that goes all the way back to my being a kid. I remember being really young (maybe five or six years old) and my mom teaching me how to play Monopoly. I lost badly and remember pouting, wanting to give up. It's been forty years since this happened to me, but I still remember my mom encouraging me to keep playing. She reminded me about the *Little Engine That Could* book by Watty Piper, teaching me to not give up. If there's a challenge in my life, my mom taught me to work at it and keep going up the mountain until I succeed and reach the top.

I took that core concept of resilience and have applied it to any challenge that comes my way. Yes, sometimes I still fail, but it's not because I didn't try my hardest. When I started training for my first marathon, I looked at the schedule and laughed. How the hell was I going to run twenty-one miles on a Sunday a few weeks before the race and then, on race day, run 26.2 miles? All of it just seemed impossible. How could my body even do that?

The trick for me was to exercise my willpower. There is power in words and in thought. I told my friends "I am going to run a marathon." I said the words, but then I tied the goal toward a motivating factor that made sense to me. I signed up to be a member of Team Lemon and agreed to raise money for Alex's Lemonade Stand Foundation so that I could raise money to help kids with cancer. I tied a personal goal with helping kids and turned the whole training process around.

Alex lived in my neighborhood, and when she was diagnosed with cancer at a very young age, she decided to sell lemonade in order to build a hospital for sick kids. I remember seeing Alex on the news and how inspired I was seeing her work so hard to help others. She passed away at eight years of age back in 2004, and her family has continued her dream by forming a foundation and has raised millions to help fund cancer research.

Back when I was training for the marathon, I had my personal goal as well as a more public goal. I wanted to help others by running. When I ran in the early morning hours, I would listen to my body, and eventually I would want to give up. I would hit a wall, wanting to stop. But over time, I found ways of just letting my mind go and relaxing. Breathing and understanding how to take in the air to calm myself made all the difference for me. When the day came for me to run twenty-one miles, I woke up on an extremely cold day in October with a chance of light snow. I suited up, got my sneakers on, and ran. About halfway through my four-hour-plus run, the snow began to fall. I love snow. I truly do, but running for more than ten miles in it, well, that's not necessarily my idea of a good time.

I wanted to give up, but two thoughts came to me.

1. When Alex was dying of cancer, she was still able to run all those lemonade stands.
2. My mind and body came up with a mantra to propel me forward.

Just like the "I know I can, I know I can" in Watty Piper's *The Little Engine That Could* book, I felt so tired that I couldn't form sentences, but one word formed in my mind. Yes.

I breathed in with two strides forward, thought "yes," then exhaled slowly, and said, "Yes." YES, YES, yes, YES, YES. I used the mantra to propel my body and legs forward. The snow hit me on my face and landed on my glasses and melted so that I had to keep cleaning them so that I could see. I look back at that training run and can't believe how much fun I had. I found a way to overcome an obstacle that I had never thought possible. Me, run twenty-one miles in the snow? Now granted, it was a light snow and only a little slush on the ground, but I did it. I used positive thought, breathing, and a mantra (Yes, yes, yes!) to win the day.

I want to be clear on something though: I did not just get up one day and run twenty-one miles and then a few weeks later 26.2 miles. It took me nearly three years of training to prepare myself to get to that point. I had a lot of mental and physical challenges that I needed to get through, but I did do it. When I started out on my quest, I focused on one goal: I just want to become more active. The goal changed over time, and eventually I decided to run a marathon. I've run the Philadelphia marathon twice and 26.2 miles on my own as a personal race to raise money for Alex's Lemonade Stand Foundation.

What does all of this have to do with writing? Everything. Discipline, willpower, and an understanding of the body are essential for me to marry my mind with my body. When I write, I sit down, use my mind, and have to type away, using my body. I need to marry two parts of me together during that time, and often my body doesn't want to physically sit down to be in the chair to write. Just like learning how to run, I needed to learn how to write. The discipline to do that takes time, effort, and patience. It just doesn't happen overnight. But I found, and hopefully it will help you, that by exercising (running, walking, whatever you can do), I could use the downtime to unconsciously think of book ideas, but it also had the added benefit of strengthening my willpower and self-esteem.

The Soul

I added this part because of what the soul means to me. I do believe there is some form of higher power out there. I don't know more than that. If you are an atheist, you might have the urge to skip this section, but I've put some thought into this and ask you to bear with me.

I believe that it's critical for my well-being to admit and understand that I need to let go of what I cannot control.

What do I mean by that?

Let's say you've worked hard, struggled, pushed, pulled, and done everything you could for a book to see the light of day, for a relationship to remain strong, or for a job offer to become reality, but whatever the reason, it all falls flat. No amount of influence or work will make the situation turn out the way you want.

I believe that in those type of circumstances I need to let go of the situation. For my inner spirit, my soul, I need to be comfortable with letting go of a situation in which I have no influence.

I take this idea from Reinhold Niebuhr's Serenity Prayer:

God, grant me the serenity to accept the things I cannot change, courage to change the things I can, and wisdom to know the difference.

These words have often helped me in my darkest hour. No matter if "God" is Christian, Hindu, Islamic, a man or a woman, it doesn't matter. And if you are an atheist, drop off the word God and chalk it up to that which is beyond your ability to control.

What does matter to me is to accept and let go of that which I cannot change, understanding that for my sanity, it's important to know the distinction between what I can change and what I can't.

My innermost self, the "me" I am working hard on achieving self-actualization, needs to be nourished in mind, body and soul. The connection to the unknown and spiritual has been an important part of my upbringing since I was a little boy. What I believe has changed over the years, but the essential core message remains true for me:

I am not all powerful. I need to understand my limits, accept that, and be at peace with that.

I believe that the soul is the symbiotic relationship between my mind and body with the essence of my personality being a mixture of the two. The neurons that fire in my brain, how my DNA is structured, and my genes make me, well, me. There is only one me in the world. Similarly, there is only one you in the world.

For me it doesn't matter if you believe in God or not, but I think it's important to ground yourself in the world around you, understanding that you do not have absolute control of your environment. The struggle in life is knowing how you'll handle the punches when they come (and they surely will).

Back in December of 2002, my wife and I shared the good news that we were expecting our first child. In January my grandfather passed away, in March my grandmother, in May my father-in-law, and in August my son came into the world. The massive change that filled our lives in 2003 hit me like a boxer on the ropes. I felt pummeled. I remember a moment of breakdown when I was painting my son's room several months before he was born. My wife had gone out and I put on a CD and Andrea Bocelli's "Time to Say Goodbye" came on. I held the paintbrush in my hand and I sang along, breaking down into tears. My father had left my mother when I was only five or six years old, and I had only seen him a handful of times since then. But I lived with my grandfather and he taught me how to play baseball, took me to the circus, and did all the things that normally a father would do with his kid.

My grandfather's passing, and then my grandmother's so quickly, hit me hard, and I had no control of those events. And then my father-in-law passed all too soon. I prayed but could find no solace. Creatively, the energy had been drained dry from my batteries. So I cried that night while painting and had a moment of peace, knowing that by letting go of the grief, feeling it, that a connection in my mind had been formed. I learned that life is sometimes not fair and I couldn't change that. I could not bring my grandparents or my father-in-law back. I could not change any of those events.

But in time, I could recharge my spirit by being good to myself. Back in 2003, I hadn't begun to run yet. I think the healing process would have gone easier for me if I had a means to process grieving through both my body and mind. My soul, the quintessential me, needed a good long time to bounce back.

There are many ways that people can find to get in touch with their spirit or inner self. For me, I found a few practical means that aren't religious and can be used by anyone. I could have added these techniques into either the mind or body sections of this chapter, but I wanted to pull them out to differentiate them from either section. Being present in one's body and mind creates a cross section of the inner self that I am calling the soul. Call it what you will, but I found the following techniques to be of great help.

When I am under stress, I find a quiet place and do the following exercise. If you're in a rush, you can do this pretty much anywhere and focus only on a few of the steps.

Practical Help to Lower Stress

Close your eyes, and take a deep breath while slowly clenching your left fist. Keep your left fist clenched tight for a few seconds and then as you exhale (slowly), release your fist. Take four seconds or so breathing in, hold two or three seconds, then exhale slowly out of your mouth while unclenching your fist. When finished, do it again.

Repeat the process with your right fist, left foot and then right foot (by bending in your toes as you inhale), clench your teeth, squeeze tight your eyes, shrug and hold your shoulders, do the same for your pelvic floor muscle (Kegel), and then lastly tighten all your muscles at once, breathing in slowly through your nose, hold a second or two, and then exhale from your mouth slowly.

I found the above exercise to not only be a fantastic stress reliever but also a way to recharge my batteries. It's a great way for me to soothe me and relax.

Light Visualization Exercise

If I have a few more minutes, I perform the following visualization technique. I lie on my back, relax and slowly breathe in through my nose. While breathing in, I imagine a warm light entering me, permeating its way through my cells, in my blood, and through my nerves, muscles, and bones. The light cleanses as it passes through me. After a few seconds, I then exhale all the darkness, hate, and stress within me. I imagine impurities streaming out of my mouth as I exhale.

I then imagine the light traveling down through my body per breath. I breathe in a few seconds, and the light goes all through my head, out my mouth, ears, and eyes, then down my throat, and through my shoulders, and I hold it there. On exhaling, all the fear and darkness within me is slowly expunged from my body. When I take my next breath, the light continues on past my shoulders, around and through my heart, and into my lungs, filling me with goodness and light. I continue doing this until the light has completed its journey all through my body and down through my toes.

I have committed not only to my writing craft but to the balance of my mind, body, and soul. I believe it is essential for me to maintain a solid balance because of the work I have ahead. The struggles I have faced are not just on my own insecurities but also are from forces outside my control in my workplace, family life, and the world around me. Setting the foundation of a stable and healthy life that incorporates not just my physical state, but my mental and spiritual as well, is the key that has helped me remain grounded when life becomes extremely challenging.

Chapter 5: Juggling the Beast

What a fancy title for a chapter title, isn't it? Maybe you might think it's a bit fantastical or I'm exaggerating. I look at my life over the last seven years and see the great change I have been forced to adapt. Being a writer has never been easy for me because of competing priorities and blurring boundary lines. Add on top of that that I started my first book when my daughter was about two years old, well, that paints a vibrant and complicated picture.

Becoming a father to two beautiful children has been one of the most precious and amazing events of my life. Yet the struggle with lack of sleep affected me greatly. I typically get six to six and a half hours of sleep a night. I trained myself to work in the morning before my kids woke because I found it to be the best time in which I would have the least disruptions.

Although my kids would go to sleep at a decent hour, I found that I had so little energy left after a full day of work that the little bit I had left was best spent on my wife and kids. I have no way to sugarcoat the juggling act that I have had to come up with to secure time to write.

At my full-time job, I'm a director who manages my team and am also involved in large web projects that I need to shepherd with hard deadlines. My day job work often blurs into my personal time when my job isn't over at normal business hours. For my wife and many of my friends and their families, long gone are the days in which work stops when you leave the office. Instead emails and work creep into the nighttime hours, creating a serious work-life balance issue.

When a website goes down in the middle of the night, my phone goes off and I need to work with the team to help bring it back online. Although it might be 2:00 a.m. in my part of the world, people in Europe or Asia are unable to access the information they need. Granted an extreme circumstance of a website going down happens infrequently, but there have been times in which I needed to work late at night or on the weekends to ensure that a deadline was met.

My full-time job is my main priority for earning the funds necessary to support my family. Although I love writing, at this point in my career as an author, I cannot live on the income earned there. Some of you might read that and worry. Yes, more and more indie writers are earning living wage incomes, but with fierce competition and a serious time limit, I have had to make a choice:

Give up on my dream and never be an author or focus on a long-term strategy, slowly building up my backlist of books as well as my reader base.

Priorities and Boundaries

My daughter is crying from an earache and won't go to sleep, my work email is blowing up over a crisis that's popped up, and my goal of finishing a book looms over me. Yes, I have been in situations like this and have had to handle a crisis at work while my kids needed me. Typically, my writing goals are then put on the back burner. Yet setting priorities and creating boundaries has been essential to my well-being. Not just as an author but as a human being. I can't always be there for my work, family, or author career. I have needed to carve out space in discrete areas of my life so that I could maintain a healthy balance among all the pushes and pulls I encounter. What I have found most complicated are the challenges in raising children. When one of our kids had a fever, either my wife or I needed to stay home from work because we were unable to send our child to daycare. With not having family local to help us, we'd trade off.

In the beginning, my wife had a more flexible schedule, and she would take the brunt, but that shifted about four years ago when I had more vacation/personal time at work so I would watch the kids (often working from home as well). A day off to watch my son or daughter when they were sick often turned into doing both working and caring for them.

When our children were no longer in daycare, then there were the near four weeks of time that our kids had off from school for holidays, spring break, and teacher service days (this doesn't count the summer time off). With my wife again working out of the house full-time, I had more vacation time and would take a week off to be with my children. But work didn't stop. Deadlines at my job did not magically go away with being off, and neither did the need to meet my own personal writing-related deadlines.

I am the type of person who likes to get work done. I don't create a massive amount of lists, but I do like to be as organized as I can without going overboard. I expect what that means for you will be different from what it does for me. When I was younger, I would take a Post-It note, write a list of things to do on it, and then stick it in front of my laptop at home. I would see the work, handle the to-dos, and accomplish what I needed.

But the beast of work, writing, research, marketing, social media, network, career development, reading, listening, and then family life came at me hard. There are only so many hours in a day, and a decision needs to be made on how to prioritize the work. I think of the pushes and pulls of my life as multiple beasts that need to be juggled.

The greatest challenge that I have found in choosing to be an author is work-life balance. I've read articles over the years on the struggle that other people have with trying to find the right balance between work and personal downtime, but when I chose to be an author, I entered into the realm of a startup mentality. Startup companies are known for being tremendously hard to run because it takes so much work to keep the company afloat. Writing in the twenty-first century isn't simply about getting a book out on paper and then handing it over to a publisher and forgetting about it.

Becoming a successful writer encompasses understanding the craft but also the business side of your new career. I went from working full-time (plus some with my off-hour work) to also launching another career in choosing to become an indie author. I did not need to just write, but I had to hire graphic designers, editors, and proofreaders, take online marketing classes, learn social media, write a business plan, devise and implement book launch campaigns, cultivate book reviews, train on bettering my writing ability, and then implement a successful email marketing campaign, create/write Facebook ads, and understand the return on investment by studying the analytics—not only of my website but of tracking my sales.

The amount of work I have needed to do is both exciting and overwhelming. I love to learn. I love reading, listening, watching, and then understanding how I can take what I have learned and apply it to my life. When I first set up my own email marketing automation flow, I had a sense of accomplishment, knowing I could learn how to create a system that would work for me in my off hours. I could be sleeping and still add people to my mailing list and send communications to new readers, offering them incentives for joining.

The beast is many headed. At this point, I don't even know how many heads the damn thing has. It's a shifting mass of protoplasm that grows back two heads after I cut off one just like a Lernaean hydra from Greek mythology.

To help, here is a breakdown of the various things I have needed to juggle. I'm not assigning an importance to them outside of family being number one.

Support Network

Family life
Extended family
Friends
Recreation, entertainment, and fun

Work

Full-time job
Conferences, webinars, and professional development

Research

Read and learn about the topic I'll be writing a book about

Writing

Sitting butt down in chair to write
Editing
Learning the craft

Business of Writing

Understanding copyright
Hiring graphic designers, copy editors, developmental editors, and proofreaders
Virtual assistants (Wish I had one!)
Learning about contracts
Keeping track of sales
Learning about whether to form an LLC or incorporating
Formatting manuscripts to various ebook formats
Taxes
Creating a business plan (yearly goals and five-year goals)

Assessing performance quarterly
Working with narrator to create audiobook

Customer Service

Responding to readers' emails
Answering tech questions about "how to" get a free book/story on an ebook device

Marketing

Book launch plan
Communication plans
Formulating call to actions (CTAs) in the fronts/backs of all my ebooks (e.g., "Get book 2 now!")
Facebook ads/tracking pixels
Bookbub
Developing strategy to cultivate book reviews and then execute
Book readings
Networking with likeminded authors to help promote each other's books
Building a close-knit street team
Writing email blasts and developing an editorial calendar about sending out the posts
Blogging on topics related to the genre I write
Updating the website

Social Media

Setting up the accounts
Learning how to use the tools
Experimenting and engaging with readers, fellow authors, and influencers

I wanted to list the main areas of work I've had to do so that you can have a good overview of the types of skills needed to be an indie author. I've stumbled, fallen, and failed, but then I got back up, wiped off my dirty knees, and started working again. Onward and upward. Onward. It's that mantra that I wrote about in the previous chapter. Yes, yes, yes. I keep moving forward to achieve my goal. But a funny thing happened over time.

Sleep deprivation, stress, competing priorities, the joy of family life (birthdays, holidays, my daughter learning how to walk, and my son reading to me for the first time)—all this crept up on me and overwhelmed me so that I lost track about why I was writing. The only important thing that mattered was to chop the hydra's head off in front of me, and when two sprang up in its place, well, then, I needed to chop those two off as well.

The work became more about tactical aspects and less on strategy, fulfillment, and self-expression. The creative spark that burned so bright in me had turned into a diamond-tipped spear I used to kill the hydra tasks in front of me. The beast begat more beasts, and I fell down a deep, black well, knowing I had to write, and if I worked hard enough, I would one day see the light of morning.

The dream of light, success, joy, and release were always out of reach, but like a tired marathoner, I struggled onward, not only slaying the beasts in front of me but then taking on new ones—well, because I guess I could.

I found it nearly impossible to continue at the speed I was going at, and here's a secret that I will share with you: I frequently became frustrated with myself when I networked with other authors who were reporting they were raking in the money. In fact, over the years, several romance authors shared that their sales had been so great that one was able to pay off her house and another her car. I took all of this in, redoubled my efforts, and buckled down, and I continued to compare my work to that of others.

Why wasn't I being as successful as other writers? Did my writing suck? I was getting good reviews. What if I branched out more? What if I reached out and did more, faster and more efficiently? When I look back, I think of two funny stories to show how desperate I was for acceptance and validation as a writer.

Several years ago, I was listening to Adam Curry's podcast (former MTV video jockey from the '90s), and he mentioned an adult film actress he had noticed using social media successfully. I looked this woman up on Twitter and learned that she loved reading fantasy. I networked with her and sent her a copy of my book. To put this in context, at this same time, I had sent books to Australia and Europe and then digital copies to more than a hundred reviewers. With the woman who worked in pornography for a living, I thought that if she liked the book, she would tweet about it, and it would help me get more readers.

I can look back and laugh at myself now at how naive and stupid the idea was. I thought if I took a risk and made contact with a person who had a following, her fans would learn about my book and then buy it. But did I really think that my feminist book, geared toward women, would find the right audience through the Twitter followers of an adult film actress? Didn't I realize at the time that this wasn't a good idea? No. I was on autopilot and not giving myself time to build a strategy, to think, test, and explore. The actress sent me her address, and I mailed her my book, but I never heard anything else from her. I share this example with you to poke fun at myself and laugh. I have made stupid mistakes and share them because I believe it's extremely important to manage your time. Instead of throwing all sorts of paint and objects at the wall to make a painting, I've found it much more helpful to sketch out a plan first than to paint what I want on the wall.

Another time that a beast took me over was when I reached out to a former colleague. She mentioned to me that she knew a group of women who had recently formed a book club and put me in connection with them. I gave several copies of my book out, and I was all happy with myself. What a great way to help get reviews on Amazon. Why didn't I think of this before?

The women in the group read the book, and then the one-star reviews started showing up on Amazon. They hated the book. One woman wrote: "This is the worst book that I have ever read. I read the first few paragraphs and hated it."

One hydra head popped up, I blindly killed it, and two more popped up in its place. My attempt to garner honest reviews for my first book in the *Cinderella's Secret Witch Diaries* series turned into a downright disaster for me. The newer reviews popped right up, and I had to accept that I had screwed up. I never asked the age of the women in the group, what genres they liked to read, or anything like that. I just heard "book club, reviews, easy way for me to move forward and build out my audience."

In the years since *Lost* was published, I've seen great five-star reviews from women I have never met, and then, on the opposite side of the spectrum, one-star reviews. Once a woman wrote about how well I had captured the female protagonist's voice and how great I was at writing women characters. Two years later, another woman wrote about how horrible I was at writing women characters. Both reviewers were people I had never met, and they had such polar opposite experiences.

In my tunnel vision, I had neglected to do the hard work (and ongoing work) of refining who my readers are and focused instead on a quick fix. Neither of these tactics worked. In fact, the book club idea actively hurt me because the one-star reviews are still there. Thankfully, I had done enough reading to know not to respond to the horrible reviews. Some writers have done that in the past, and they've been brought down by their own readers for fighting with them.

When I had blinders on, I only saw the beast, tried to juggle, and then killed more beasts. I didn't have a plan, a strategy, a means, for handling all of the work and also building in time to rest and relax. I just plowed onward, using my force of will to keep on moving forward. I would not give up. I would not only triple my efforts but learn new and exciting things and apply that to what I already knew. I would succeed no matter what. I would make it all come to be, and I would reach that holy place in the sky in which I would be known as "an author of worth." I'd make it and really be someone. If I just worked harder, kept my nose to the grindstone, and focused, I knew I could make it. I just knew it!

I can feel you cringing through the page as you're reading this. You know it. You can see that I was headed onward like a runaway train rushing toward the wall. Burnout waited for me with his wily fingers that clicked like needles in the dark of night, like a sentient beast who would not only take my creativity from me but my sanity as well.

Chapter 6: The Truth About Burnout

I know that I might offend you by saying this, but I want to be honest. I do not believe in writer's block. I just don't believe that it exists. What I do believe is that I have encountered resistance before and have wanted to give up.

When I was about halfway through writing *Lost*, I flitted along, and an interesting thing happened. The holidays were coming, and I was busy with work and family life, and I wanted to give myself some time off. I stopped writing for a few weeks, and the holidays came and went. I had a great time, and then I just didn't want to get back to writing. I knew it was going to be difficult to sit down and stare at the blank page so I pushed the work off. January came and another week or two went by, and I had to make a decision: Was I a writer or did I simply want to say that I want to write? I hit the wall head on and needed to wrestle with my feelings.

In my head, the con list went something like this: "I'm working really hard at my job and then some! I'm successful, managing people, have to travel for work soon, and will be seriously swamped for work. And raising two kids, that also takes a lot of work. I don't really have to do this."

That poison started to creep into my consciousness, and I just let things slide for a bit. But then I started thinking about what I had promised myself and how I had told my family and friends that I was writing a book. At the moment, I wasn't. I had stopped. I had given up under the pretense that I needed a little bit of time to refresh, restart my batteries, and to clear the air a bit.

I do not remember the exact day when I changed my mind, but I do recall that I got up one morning and set my laptop up at the kitchen table. Outside there was a light blanket of snow on the ground. I forced myself to sit down to write, and there were times when I would look up and fear came over me. What should I write next? I didn't know what to do. I feared that I had run out of ideas and had hit this crazy wall in front of me. I had no words. I had hit a blockade.

I was tired, exhausted, and spent from work, family life, and the holidays—I had hit the doldrums of winter and just wanted to throw my hands up in the air and toss all my hopes and dreams away. But I didn't. I faced my fear. Now when I come up against a block like that, I have a better idea of what to do. I think of a problem, a question, an idea, and start to write about it. There's book work and there's prep work to help me unleash my creativity.

For example, if I'm blocked, I now know I can do several things. I can simply sit down and write about how I feel. Or I can write to a trusted friend. Just let all the angst out of me and write about my inner feelings and why I am stuck.

Sometimes that doesn't work. I also have found a way to overcome resistance to writing by simply putting the project down and switching gears and writing something else. When I have been structured for a long time in writing a specific project, I have found that giving myself the freedom to write something else can be extremely helpful. A blog post or an article is sometimes exactly what I need to help me relax and get over myself. What I have found helpful is that I look at my problem and break it apart. If I'm writing a book, I can sit down and say: "I have ninety thousand more words to write." Or, I could say: "Today, I only need to write fifteen hundred words." There is a big difference between focusing on today instead of being overwhelmed by the sheer immensity of the work in front of me.

By breaking down the challenge ahead into bite-sized pieces, I'm better able to overcome the resistance and find a way to move forward and reach my goal.

But that's the smart way of going about things, the healthy way. With burnout, I'm going to take you on a dark journey that I stumbled down more than once. In looking back at the books I wrote, I think *Lost* was the hardest. I wrote *Dorothea's Song* when I was sixteen years old and then rewrote it multiple times up through my twenties. *Lost* was different. It took me eighteen months from concept to holding the print version in my hand. That was an extremely long amount of time. I know that many professional writers can complete a book in a month or two.

When I learned about the habits of other writers, I took that hard. I just did not see how it was possible to get that much work done so quickly. I thought that maybe something was wrong with me. Maybe I didn't know what I was doing (well, part of that was true) and needed a way to regroup and push forward. For *Stolen* (book two in my *Cinderella's Secret Witch Diaries* series), I knocked the time down to twelve months. I had a better idea of how to plot, move the story forward, and complete the tasks necessary for me to finish up faster.

Fast-forward to book three in the series, *Found*, and I slipped back to sixteen months' worth of work. Keep in mind that during this time I worked full-time and raised my kids with my wife. My daughter was about to turn seven back in 2014 and my son eleven. I had a lot on my plate both personally and professionally. Back in 2012, I had moved to a new day job and had a larger responsibility with more hours and several extremely exciting, yet challenging, projects to complete.

Found was extremely difficult for me to write because I realized during the second draft of the book that about a third of it needed to be thrown out. Why? The storyline of one of the main characters just wasn't working. I had to take a step back and plan what to do. Emotionally and psychologically, I felt like I had been punched in the gut. I struggled with balancing work and family but now had the challenge of finding a way to finish my third book—all while I was still learning marketing techniques to sell my first two books. I saw no end in sight for the work. I just couldn't figure out how to move forward.

I stopped writing for several weeks and had no energy. I kept wondering how I was going to finish *Found*. I just didn't see how it was possible because I dreaded sitting down with a Word file and then going through scene by scene, cutting out the ones that dealt with a central character, rewriting those scenes, and then rethreading the book all together again. The amount of work ahead of me seemed insurmountable. How was I going to do the work? I meant literally: How?

A Way Forward

Burnout can be described as an exhaustive state in which you have no energy left to provide credible creative input. You're spent, drained, and just want to sit on the floor and stare at a wall. And that's okay, well, for a little while at least. What I know now are the warning signs and how to address them in a practical matter. But when I hit the burnout phase, I typically take one of these two paths forward:

1. Speed up and crash through the burnout into the extremely fun and dangerous territory of meltdown (more on that in the next chapter)
2. Stall and give up

Neither option is helpful in the long run. However, I found that taking a few days off (a weekend or long weekend) to assess the problem has helped me immensely in the past. The only issue is that I often found that if I gave myself too much time off (more than a week), then I simply resisted and didn't want to get back to work. Each day past a week off makes it harder and harder for me to remember the connective tissue of the story and how to thread that creatively into the re-animation of my living, breathing manuscript. But if I take a step back, reflect and admit to myself what the problem is, I often find that I can solve the issue pretty easily.

Some helpful tips I have discovered to help me get out of the burnout cycle:

- Exercise. When I run, walk, do gardening work, or even clean bathrooms, the physical activity changes my brain. The endorphins that surge through me when I exercise help inspire me and allow different neurons in my brain to fire off. Exercise is the number one means for me to deal with burnout and see a path forward.
- Talk it out. I have two close friends with whom I can share my writing concerns with without fear of being judged. I meet them for dinner or lunch and then simply talk.
- Get the right tools. I never quite understood this when I first started writing books. Now when I look back, I don't know how I just used Microsoft Word to write my books. Having one huge document to capture up to 110,000 words was pretty insane. Now I use a mixture of Google Docs and Scrivener. With Google Docs, I create a folder for each chapter and then a separate Google document for each scene. Same thing with Scrivener. Breaking up my book into pieces, allows me to easily manipulate it. I can throw away a whole chapter, a set of chapters, or just certain scenes and regroup those scenes/chapters into a "throw away" folder. If I change my mind, I can bring the deleted chapters back without any fuss. For me, past burnout came when I was juggling so many things and then hit a wall and did not know how to solve the problem in front of me. I would shut down, stew in a funk, and just want to give up.

- Write it out. When I was younger, I used to journal all the time. I'd sit in front of a computer and let my fingers flit away. Such free-form writing allowed me to connect my ideas with how I could translate those thoughts into words. In fact, my favorite type of writing is free-form writing. It's healing for me as I can express my feelings, let them out on a page (without any judgment), and then come back and get back to work.

- Sing it out. I am my mother's son. When growing up, I saw my mom deal with her divorce by putting on loud music and belting the song out. She released her frustration and anger by singing along with the music. I've picked up that trait, and people often think I'm crazy, but I find it extremely therapeutic to release my angst by singing. A good Beatles or Indigo Girls song is often just the right thing to help me. (Note: I never admitted that I was good at singing, but I enjoy it!)

- Meditate and breathe. I went over this in an earlier chapter, but it's worth mentioning here. When I am stuck, clearing my mind of my worries and focusing simply on breathing helps put me into an open state. Once I am open to change or a solution, I often find that I'm extremely capable of helping myself out of the rut I'm in. I simply need to create the space in my life for a solution, and then one often presents itself. I am amazed at how when I'm exercising or meditating that a solution presents itself to me when I truly listen to my body. Sometimes the answer doesn't come right away, but if I'm patient, then the answer always does come to me.

The tips I listed have helped me when I needed to reset and get back on course. What I learned is that I need to be self-aware of my state of mind and be ready to adjust my behaviors and mindset when needed. To help, let me take a step back.

Warning Signs

There have been times in the last seven years when I wake up and realize that I'm on auto-pilot. I work, eat, sleep, do my chores, and realize I'm not taking time to enjoy those precious moments that, in the future, I'll look back and smile on. Sometimes it's the little things like working with my daughter, teaching her how to plant tomatoes, and then watering them each night with her when I get home from work. Even though she doesn't like eating raw tomatoes, it's fun to work with her and teach her how to tend a garden. Or when my son comes to me and talks to me about a new app that's out, explaining what he thinks about it. When I'm not making time for the things that really matter in life, it's usually the number-one sign that I'm headed toward a burnout.

Listen

The question that I often need to ask myself is: Am I truly listening to my family? When they talk to me, am I more focused on the next few minutes afterward? I'm being honest here and ask that you do the same. With so few hours in the day, and even less free time, I found that the struggle between trying to get work done often blurs into my private family time. Often this is a sign that I've lost my way. If I'm not making time to listen to my own flesh and blood, what the hell am I doing?

I've been working on being more present with my family. When my son or daughter comes to me, if I'm in the middle of a work crisis (this happens when a website is down), I'll respectfully tell them that I'm busy and will make time for them later. But when I do make that time, then I ensure that I make eye contact with them, stop whatever else I'm doing, and be open to receiving communication from them.

The challenge for me is that there's that little voice in my head that says, "You have one thousand and one things yet to do and only so much time. How are you going to do all the work? Focus on the work. If you want to be successful, then focus on that!"

That little voice is a liar though. Being so focused on work doesn't allow me to participate fully in my life and traps me within a mess of deadlines without any hope of true intimacy with people. Who wants to be around someone who is only grudgingly listening to you? No one. But by opening up the lines of communication and truly listening to those around me, well, new doors are opened. I actually get to learn new things and get to build a bond with the people in my life. Always working and trying to complete "the next task" sets me up for failure because there will always be something else to do.

Sleep

I typically get six to seven hours of sleep each night. I'm a creature of habit in that I fall asleep around the same time each night and my body wakes me up the same time each day. I don't use an alarm clock because my body has been waking me up for decades.

But there are times when I need to work late or go to work early. If I'm stuck at work until 9:00 p.m., having been there since the early morning, the rest of my day has to be put aside. I cannot make more hours. Instead, I come home, focus on spending time with my family, and call it a day. Yet at times, I have pushed onward by either staying up late to get some work done or, more my taste these days, I get up early. I've had to run at 4:30 a.m. before work in order to train for a marathon. It's not fun, but I needed to pull back on sleep.

Over the long term, losing sleep is extremely bad for me. After two days of less than five hours of sleep, I start going through life in a fog. I have a difficult time making decisions, my paranoid radar goes up, and I am grumpy with a short fuse.

Sleep not only heals the body, but I'm also clearer, more focused, and can handle stress better when I'm rested. I used to think that I needed to stay up to get work done, but if I have been up since 4:30 a.m. and am falling asleep by 9:30 p.m., then I go to bed. Sleep is my friend.

But a good night of sleep is also a great way for me to subconsciously work on ideation. Over the years, I have had dreams (sometimes nightmares) that became the seeds of novels and short stories. Granted, dreaming up new ideas doesn't happen that often for me, but it's happened enough that I still remember decades out a few dreams that had such an effect on me that I thought the dream to be real.

If you're not sleeping enough, take the time to listen to your body. To be honest, I found it difficult to do that myself, but over time, I realized that when I'm rested, not only am I more productive, but I'm a happier person, and my family really, really likes that!

Eating

What do I eat? How much I eat and how often are key to not only keeping my body healthy but in training for a marathon. When I ran my first marathon, it dawned on me that I would be running for five hours straight and that I needed to take in food during that time. I could not simply will myself to run. I needed energy. During my training, I learned what worked for me and what didn't. Through trial and error, I discovered that if I ate well, not only would I heal faster from sore legs but taking in fresh vegetables and protein would also help build muscle. If I didn't eat well, then I suffered.

Before I started running, I never really stopped to think about the connection between what I eat, what impact it had on me, and how this affected me over time. I would eat whatever I wanted. I had a fast metabolism and figured I'd be fine. Was I eating enough protein? Too much carbs? Way too much sugar? I've been more mindful of my diet because I want to take care of my body.

For me, I need to eat every six to eight hours. If I don't, I have a difficult time making decisions and feel jittery. My blood sugar level drops, and if I don't eat soon, then I am not as productive as I'd like. My head races and I start making stupid mistakes.

There's also the difference between eating (e.g., shoveling food into my mouth) and being social with other people and eating. At work, I fail at this daily. Usually I eat quickly while working at my desk. But when I take time to go eat with friends, I'm forced to get up, relocate from my desk, come out of my introverted shell, and focus on making connections with people and eating.

I've learned over the years what foods are good for me (hint: they're green and leafy) and how to incorporate better eating habits into my life. The older I get, the slower my metabolism, and I discovered much of what I ate wasn't healthy. I've changed all of that slowly over time. Do I still fall down and eat junk sometimes? Yes. I'm not going to lie to you. But on a typical morning, I make my own protein shake with fresh kale leaves. I'm not eating sugary cereal, and I make certain I am taking in more fruits and vegetables throughout the day.

Drink

This one might be tricky for some. About twenty years ago, I started having massive headaches related to caffeine withdrawal. I was in graduate school at the time and would stay up until the sun rose. To keep me up all night, I'd drink several cherry Cokes while hanging out with friends. I'd drink the soda sometimes until 3:00 a.m. and stay up until the sun rose. I went to school and worked at night so I'd sleep sometimes until 11:00 a.m., do my school work, and head out the next night. But the caffeine started catching up with me. The more soda I drank, the sooner I'd get my headaches. Then one day I just stopped drinking soda cold turkey. I had headaches for a few days, but then I went to feeling fine.

I started drinking hot green tea in the morning (I never got into coffee.) and have water during the day. I also cut out the fruit drinks I used to drink because they all contained too much sugar.

After I started to run, I needed to work in more water to my drinking each day so that I could remain hydrated. I also discovered a correlation between drinking alcohol and my running performance as well as the length of my recovery time from a long run. I'm a lightweight when it comes to alcohol. If I have two drinks, I'm fine.

The biggest challenge was giving up caffeine. Over the years, coworkers and friends have had their own challenges with struggling against the caffeine beast. It's not an easy one to break. I'm not saying to stop drinking coffee, but I simply wanted to share how adverse of an effect caffeine was having on me and what I did to stop that.

The Burnout Clues

When I look back at my difficult times, I can point to several warning signs. Maybe I wasn't sleeping right, eating or drinking properly, or listening to other clues that my body was sending to me. I often would ignore all the warning signs and try to push through. Did that work for me? Yes, it did a few times, but in the long run, I often felt run down and extremely tired.

Now I have a nice and simple trick to help me take an inventory on myself. When I'm starting to get stressed out and I see several of the warning signs pop up, I ask:

Is this healthy for me?

Whatever the situation or problem I'm facing, I ask myself that question. If yes, then I continue doing the work. If no, then I work on stopping as soon as I can. Asking myself if the activity I'm doing is healthy for me isn't an easy thing to do. Sometimes I don't like the answer I get and keep doing the work anyway. That's not smart of me, but who says I'm always smart?

Case in point: Back in 2015, I wanted to try something new and different. I had completed the first three books of the *Cinderella's Secret Witch Diaries* series and wanted to start a new one. I had been networking with several writers and learned how several romance writers were cranking out four or more books a year. These writers were building up a readership and had big numbers to prove that all their hard work was working for them.

With all this in mind, I came up with the idea of writing a book in the month of January 2015. I had missed out on National Novel Writing Month (NaNoWriMo) the previous November but thought I'd simply take the month of January to crank a book out. The plan was to launch book one in a series early in the year and then publish book two a few short months after that. I came up with the plan, set to work, and pushed hard to meet my objectives.

Keep in mind that I still worked full-time, was raising a family, and struggled with learning marketing as well as started to network more. I took it all on. What "it" was, I couldn't say for sure, but I threw myself into my work. Instead of listening to my body, taking time to reflect or doing anything that would be helpful to my current state, I chose to ignore all the warning signs around me and push onward.

I expect you have had similar times in your life in which you're up against a struggle and you decide to "push through."

Pushing Through

Makes sense on the surface, doesn't it? I'm running a marathon and want to push through any pain. There's a deadline coming up and you push through to make it. Neglecting to eat, sleep, or take care of your most basic needs.

I can easily struggle and use my willpower to overcome a rough time. I've actually trained myself through running long miles how to put myself into a trance-like state to focus my energy to complete my run. But when I push through too often, I neglect to keep the "Is this healthy for me?" voice alive. Burnout can come in many forms. It can be short lived (if you catch it fast), mid-lived if neglected, or escalated to a full-on meltdown if not caught and addressed.

My friends, family, and my own inner voice are meant to be set up to be touchstones to help me when the going gets rough. But a funny thing happens when you're taking on too much work: Instead of stopping to listen to those around me, I isolated myself with my work and experienced tunnel vision, focusing only on the work and the limited view of the world around me. I believed that if I spent enough energy and focused myself on the task that I could push through to succeed. My sheer will could break through any barrier. People would have to see how good my writing was, right?

When I'm burned out, I know that I come to a spot in which I don't care anymore. I have no more energy, and my creativity is either zapped or resistant. I find myself pulled in ways that I cannot fully understand, and with sleep deprivation, I'm not making smart choices.

I still remember feeling exhausted and burned out while writing *Found*. I just didn't want to finish the book. Thankfully, I did give myself some time to relax, rethink my strategy, and then came back to the work fairly quickly.

But in 2015, I pushed through, forcing myself to deal with work, family, and my writing problems all at once. I went to light speed on my work and had my blinders on full. Nothing would stop me, and I would burn like a brilliant sun because I knew that I could succeed. (See anything wrong with that?) I went right out of the stratosphere from burnout into meltdown mode. I joke a bit about it now, but it's simply a mechanism I'm using to help me cope with how badly I behaved. I share this with you carefully so as to use my experience to help remind me of where I have come but to also show you what can happen when we do not stop and address feelings of burnout. Meltdown is not fun. It's selfish, petty, and goes against everything that I believe, but I ignored all that and went right into the storm full on.

Chapter 7: Meltdown

In January of 2015, I completed *Awakenings* (book one in the *Witch's Coven* series). I wrote more than 1,500 words a day, worked full-time at my day job, and somehow juggled family, chores, and life problems. After I finished book one, I rushed forward and started planning out *Betrayals*, book two.

After I finished *Awakenings*, I edited it quickly, formatted the book, had the cover designed, and continued to learn marketing by building up my email list, and I released the book in May 2015. My darkest time and meltdown took place in mid-February.

I think the best way to describe what I was going through isn't to blame away my behaviors on lack of sleep, a tunnel vision, or my inability to listen to my own body but to accept that I was in the wrong.

Financially, my wife and I were going through an extremely difficult time, and we were fighting often. My kids were seeing the effects of our arguing, and I kept blaming everyone around me. I thought, Why isn't everyone as organized as I am? Why do I have to do everything myself? I'm working and then working a second career on top of that, but I still am making time to clean, cook, and do the chores. With my day so planned out, I had no free time to chit-chat or smell the roses.

I woke up early, lost sleep, went to work, either cleaned up from dinner or cooked it (depending on the night), and took my turn putting the kids to bed. I had a schedule, damn it, and I was ready to go. The straw that broke the camel's back came when a mistake had been made on our taxes. My wife and I realized we owed a tremendous amount of money to the Internal Revenue Service. We had the funds to cover it, but I lost it. I simply wanted to lash out because I felt superior. My wife and I fought over the money, and I blamed her for the taxes mistake. Instead of working the problem out, I did not accept that a mistake was made and move on. We fought and I resented the fact that I carried the weight of the world on my shoulders. All I saw was me, me, and me. Now when I write this, and look back, I feel ashamed.

The money problem wasn't the issue. At the core was my resentment that my family was holding me back (or so I thought at the time) from succeeding in my author career. I took out all my anger and frustration on my family. Unfortunately, my wife took the brunt of my anger. She and I were supposed to be celebrating twenty years of being together, but I screwed up and made the month of February the worst in our entire time together.

In short, I acted like an asshole, yelling, arguing, and being smug. I put all the blame on my wife, and instead of taking a step back to see that I was pushing myself too hard, I refocused my frustration and anger toward her. That bled over toward our kids as they saw how we fought, and at the end of it all, what did I have to show? I nearly lost my marriage.

I finally understood some of what my father and mother must have been going through before they separated and eventually divorced. Instead of having my best friend by my side, we went to being enemies. I could not extract myself from my goals to slow down, take a break and refill my tired spirit. I was angry that I wasn't seeing the success I thought I should have by publishing more books, and all my hard work resulted in little sales. The taxes problem compounded all of my fears and blew up in my face.

The greatest mistake that I made was to ignore all the warning signs around me. My fuse was short, I wasn't happy, I could not rest without thinking that a clock was ticking, and I always thought I was wasting time when a problem came before me.

I could not see how I could break out of the vicious cycle that I had fallen into. So I pushed onward until everything fell apart. Our marriage hung in the balance. After the big arguments between my wife and me, she asked me to go to couple's counseling to find a way to deal with our problems. I'll be a bit vulnerable here and won't share the gory details, but I think it's important to be honest. I was resistant to change at first. I was in my own little mind bunker, hunkered down and ready to take on the apocalypse. In my sleep-deprived state, I thought I was doing the work I needed to do. I understood that being an author meant hard work, would take years and dedication, and I wanted to prove to myself that I could make it and be successful. Yes, I had an extremely good full-time job that paid me well, but I felt broken, angry, and distraught that I was having such little financial success. After my wife asked me to go to counseling, I took some time to reflect on my behavior and came to the conclusion that I had my priorities all messed up. If I wanted to have a happy life (and marriage), then I needed to take the first step.

Acceptance

First, I needed to admit I had screwed up. I had sacrificed everything in the hopes of achieving glory, becoming a best-selling author, and on hoping that my writing would help inspire millions. But the reality was much different from my dreams. By pushing myself too hard, I severely damaged the relationship between my wife and me, and I wasn't being truly present with my kids. In fact, the reason why I started writing the *Cinderella's Secret Witch Diaries* series was for my daughter, but by not modeling good behavior for her and my son, I defeated the whole purpose of what I wrote.

I tried, and failed, at being the best father, husband, son, coworker, friend, and author. I cleaned, cooked, ran, worked, wrote, and rushed around like a chicken without a head as my grandmother used to say. I exhausted my own reserves, pushed past the safety limits, and lost touch with all that I loved so much.

Other writers have talked about their struggles, addictions, and problems, but all of that seemed so distant to me. I thought I had it all figured out, believing I could make something happen by forcing it to be. If I willed it, struggled for it, I could make it become reality. The funny thing is that Cinderella in my books tries so hard to do the same thing. She also fails and doesn't see her path for quite some time.

Until I said the words "I can't do it all," I wasn't truly accepting my situation. I needed to face myself in the mirror and admit that I needed a drastic change, reorient my life, stop, assess, and then create a plan.

Why do I share this? I want to lay bare where I screwed up, admit to that and, as I like to do, share my story with people so that maybe others might see my story as a cautionary tale.

Climbing Out of the Hole

After I finished *Awakenings* and *Betrayals* in 2015, I switched gears by reflecting on my life and making drastic changes. I needed more sleep, more time to play, exercise, spend time with my kids and wife and yet still achieve my writing goals. When I went through my darkest time, I never wanted to quit writing entirely. I knew I needed to pull back and realized that writing a novel in a month, then quickly publishing that book, and knocking out a second, with all the other work I did, wasn't going to be sustainable.

I went to counseling with my wife and learned better communication skills and how to be a better listener. I'll need to keep working on that for the rest of my life. What I learned is that life isn't so simple. I cannot simply "set it and forget it."

To be a good partner, I need to continually work on my own struggles and apply what I learn about myself to my family and the rest of the world. The best analogy I can think of is a physical one. After I tore my Achilles tendon a few years back, I could not believe that in six short weeks I had lost the ability to walk. I had gone from running a marathon to not being able to walk across the room once my tendon had healed. I had to relearn how to walk and slowly rebuild the muscle back up with exercise.

The same is true of my marriage, relationship with my kids, and my interactions with everyone else. I needed to exercise my listening and communication skills. I cannot sit back and coast. Marriage isn't like that. And if you have kids, then I need not say more. You understand where I'm coming from in the challenges of raising another human being in your household.

I had prided myself in being a good listener (My wife would honestly and without malicious intent wholeheartedly disagree.), but I only saw what I could see with the blinders I had on. If I am honest with myself, I can see that I often put myself into a hole emotionally to distance myself from the world so that I could tap into my creativity, focus, and get the writing work done. It's great that I can work hard but not to the detriment of my family life.

Instead of seeing myself in a pit and needing to climb out of it, I've turned the concept around in my head. By being more present and willing to focus on my own interpersonal skills, I'm choosing to have a more fulfilling and robust life. Some days I succeed in being a good listener and on others I fail. But I keep moving forward.

Beating Yourself Up

I would not be surprised if you work full-time, have a family, and are an author that guilt pops up in your life every now and again. I grew up in an Italian/Irish Catholic family and guilt hung heavy over us. Many of the decisions my family made were tied closely to guilt.

And when I've felt guilty, I often then beat myself up emotionally. I put myself down, thinking I could do better.

In the middle of my meltdown, what fueled the nuclear fission was the recycling of an unhealthy thought process. I wanted to be a successful writer but realized I couldn't do it as quickly as I would like. I had commitments to my family and work. The competing priorities sometimes became jumbled in my mind, and the line between what I actually needed to do to remain healthy became blurred.

I could not be at every art show or middle of the day holiday skit for my kids. But I could be at some of those events while at other times I needed to be away working at a conference across the country for up to nine days. That happened three or four times a year for about eight years of my son's life, and that put a major stress on my wife.

I remember one time when I was in San Francisco, and I called home to see how my wife was doing. I had worked from 5:00 a.m. until 7:00 p.m., but when I phoned my wife on the East Coast, it was 10:00 p.m. there and we used to call it the witching hour. I heard both my kids crying in the background, and I could not do much to help. I felt guilty, sad that so much distance separated us, and longed to get home.

To help, I created short videos that I sent to my kids and learned they liked to play them over and over again. Years later, roles reversed and my wife needed to travel. Our kids were a bit older, and the struggle of the early years had changed more into the obstinate attitude of pre-teens. Instead of feeling guilt, I better understand my wife's tiredness and the hard work she had put in to raise our kids when I had been away. Now I needed to be the one with the two screaming kids (Well, it was their fighting more than crying.) while my wife called and mentioned how she needed to head out to a fancy restaurant for a late work meeting.

Instead of beating myself up with guilt over what I could be there for, or what I didn't do, the different perspective of my being at home while my wife was away helped me better understand that my taking positive actions would be more beneficial in the long run than closing down and feeling guilty.

I Can't Do It All

I simply can't. Accepting my limitations isn't easy for me because I believe that if I put my nose to the grindstone then I can overcome any challenge. I just need to be persistent. Being an author in the twenty-first century is much more involved than sitting down, writing, editing, and then sending my book out to a publishing house. I opted for a much more interesting, yet complex, path. By choosing to be an indie author, I'm my own publisher. I've created my own business and need to oversee all aspects of it. I need to hire other creative people (copyeditors, designers, narrators, etc.) and do a laundry list of other things. The sheer amount of work I need to do sometimes overwhelms me.

Or, as I like to do with my wife, I'd like to enumerate all the work I've done. By clearing that off my chest, I can understand that I am moving forward on my goals. Though I'm working on being mindful to not overshare with my wife and friends. I can't imagine anything more mind-numbing than to listen to me talk about the million and one things I've done in my writing career. But the reality remains: No matter how much I do accomplish, I can't do it all.

I need time to reflect. The challenge is understanding that in the moment. It's great that I can write about all of this from my current reflective state, but how am I going to get out of the next time I start to slip and lose my way?

Practical Tips

In recovering from my Achilles tendon injury, on day two I took a Post-It note and stuck it right on my monitor. It simply read:
"Be positive."
Each morning, I'd get up, see the note, and reflect on why I put that there. I'm a visual person and find a simple reminder to be extremely helpful to nudge me in the right direction. I've also put other inspirational quotes up. Another one that I've already shared that is extremely helpful for me is:
"Is this healthy for me?"
Try the notes. Don't try ten notes at once, but start small and be honest with yourself. The tips I share here are meant to be easy to try and use. There's no magic involved in any of this. But the work is hard and requires a willingness to change.

Over time I have taken a hard look at my goals and where I want to end up. I might never achieve the success that I dream of as a writer, but I now focus more on the connection with my readers. When I write, I imagine that I am having a nice fireside chat with my reader.

We sit by the fire, I sip a glass of ice water with lemon and we talk. I listen and share, and afterward, we leave feeling a sense of connection.

To get to that place, I've chosen a holistic approach, focusing on my body, mind, and soul. I've gone through the importance of those parts in a previous chapter, but I wanted to share that I'm continually looking to learn more. I read books about writing, self-improvement, and marketing and also listen to podcasts. I've chosen to surround myself with positive influences as well as people. The work that I've set out to do is a mindful path on the road of life. Yes, I know that sounds a bit much, but I'm on the proverbial "road less traveled." Or at least I like to think of it that way.

Coming down off my high horse, I want to learn more about life, my own, how to be a better person, and then to write entertaining books to engage my readers in stories that are inspiring.

The challenge is the juggle and remaining open to change.

Chapter 8: Finish What You Started

Beginnings are easy. Over the decades, I have had many, many creative ideas, and I learned something about myself when I was in my twenties. If I have a story idea, I need to strike when the iron is hot. If I write the idea down, but then don't actually write, I lose the idea, and my excitement wanes over time, and nothing ever comes of the project.

It is easy to come up with an idea, but seeing the idea from its infancy to a post-book launch is another story entirely. There are two major mistakes I have committed over my time as an author, and I'd like to share them with you.

I wrote *Dorothea's Song* when I was sixteen years old. I tried for a long, long time (decades) submitting the book to publishers, but I met rejection every time. Back in the '90s, before there was indie publishing, I had to follow the big publishing house rules. I tried both agents and publishers directly, but in general I had to write a query letter, a synopsis, submit the first few chapters of my book and then follow the cardinal law of traditional publishing: Don't submit the work simultaneously to other agents/publishers (Again, this was the '90s.).

My twenties flew by, and toward the end of my thirties, I stumbled into the world of indie publishing. I had found a way for my first book to see the light of day. Warts and all, the novel of my youth made it to book form. I had struggled, fought rejection, and failed more times than I could remember, but at the end of the day, I held up my book and patted myself on the back for my success.

But there's a secret here that is hiding beneath the surface. I wrote the first draft of *Dorothea's Song* in the late '80s, rewrote it several times in the '90s, and then published it back in 2007. So, what's the problem? I never had the guts to write more books. I never finished what I started. Instead of championing one novel, which I foolishly thought would be a bestseller, I could have started another series or even written additional books in the world of The Realms I had created in *Dorothea's Song*.

Back in the late '90s, I did write a sequel to my first book, but that's never seen the light of day. I have a rough draft of a novel, but I never did anything with it. Why? That's a really good question. I stupidly believed the publishing giants would discover me and pull me out of obscurity so the world would see what a great writer I truly was. I wrote one book, hung all my hopes and dreams on that book, and had no idea what else I would do with my life. I imprisoned myself to think that, unless my first book was published and successful, I couldn't write a sequel. And if I couldn't write book two in the series, then how was I supposed to come up with another great world to create? I had already created one world, there were only so many ideas, and I just didn't know what I would do from there.

No One Need Validate You But You

The hard lesson that took me decades to learn is so simple, but it was extremely hard to put into practice. I needed to believe in myself as an author. And I didn't. Yes, *Dorothea's Song* is not as good as my most recent book. When I look back at all the times I submitted *Dorothea's Song* to agents and publishers, I remember taking the rejections as personal failures, and over time, I gave up hope. It would take months to hear back from agents, who would send me a rejection form letter (or occasionally a personalized one), and then I'd simply send the book out to another agent or publisher and so on and so on. During the waiting periods, I'd hoped to be inspired by a magical muse, and when a new idea came to me, I'd write a short story, but I didn't know how to write another book. I just thought that I must write a sequel, and I eventually did, yet I couldn't see how I could get book two published if book one was still not helping me find success.

I believed that only outside influences could validate me to others as a writer. I put my hopes, dreams, and self-worth in the hands of people I had never met. Agents would know who was good and who wasn't. And the publishing house, well, they had to know how best to cut the wheat from the chaff. To be honest, I look back and feel regret. I wasted many years for something that never came to be. The only reason I changed is because I learned that the publishing industry was going through a dramatic revolution, and I chose to step off the traditional publishing train, opting to follow the indie publishing route. I'd rather my book be available to the world than sit on a hard drive on my computer. Better to fail, learn, and become a better writer than to accept defeat and give up my dream.

Now my self-worth rests with me. I do not need a publishing house to validate me and tell me I'm worthy of having a book published. Anyone can do that now. That's the good and the bad news.

I can write a book and publish it as often as I like, but I also need to market the book and find ways of selling it. Over the last few years, I've learned that marketing is much more difficult to do than writing a book.

My Dirty Little Secret

Now I understand I never finished what I started. I wrote my first book but then gave up. I allowed myself and identity as a writer to be imprisoned by faceless individuals and companies I have never met. It's ludicrous when I think back. I would spend money on one of the guides to literary agents and publishing houses, searching for my genre. I'd find the few names listed there, and like a dutiful student, I would follow the instructions to send them my manuscript. And then wait. And wait some more.

Instead of writing my next book or brainstorming up another series, I put all my eggs in one basket, and that was that. It's hard for me not to feel really bummed about what I chose to do because I wasted so many years doing nothing. In the last seven years, I wrote seven novels. Imagine how many I could have written over nearly twenty years!

I can't take back the past, but I can learn from it and share my experiences with you.

I wasted a lot of time looking for external validation instead of honing my craft, developing new book ideas, and continuing to write. Writing a book, for most, isn't a simple affair. I didn't just sit down, write, and with a flourish of some pixie dust, the book just sprung forth from my head. I spent years learning how to write, reading, and linking like-minded ideas to come up with plots that were exciting and fun. I wrote my first story, entitled *The Mission*, when I was nine years old. I still have the original copybook with my horribly handwritten story, complete with lots of "Pows!," "Booms!" and "Zaps!," as though I had written a comic book. And the artwork that coincides with the story is horrible. But I was nine. I look at that story, at how free I was back then, unencumbered by the weight of expectations and the world, and I can still remember the pure joy I experienced when I allowed myself to write and just be free. I let my imagination wander and had fun in writing.

That's the dirty little secret: I waited too long for others to validate me as a writer and suppressed my own joy in writing. I wrote that first story for fun, and over the years, I wrote many other stories until I wrote *Dorothea's Song* when I was sixteen. I allowed myself to climb a mountain without knowing what I was doing. When I finished the book and realized it was more than 110,000 words, I felt as though I stood on Mount Everest and didn't know what to do next. So I did what any other creative person does: I went to college.

Once I had my English literature and French degrees, I then went on to graduate school to get my master's degree. All along I kept waiting for someone to validate me for what a great writer I was. I'd submit short stories, some poems, but I didn't see that spending so much time and money to get my degrees, saying that I was a scholar, wasn't the same thing as being a writer.

I know many people who have worked really hard for their master of fine arts degree, and they haven't finished a book yet. There's a psychological barrier that needs to be overcome in getting over one's fear of failure and to put one's work out in the world. As a writer, you either find a way to beat this fear or you don't.

What I've learned, the hard way, is that writing is not easy. It takes lots of work, reading, dedication, and the desire to fail and then pick yourself up off the ground. But the really important thing that I learned is to allow yourself to dream and create new worlds along with new possibilities.

Write as Many Books as You Can

When I finished my first book, the most logical thing for me to do next was to write the next one. But I didn't. And then twenty-two years later, I wrote and published *Lost: Cinderella's Secret Witch Diaries*. I finished *Lost* and do you know what I did next? I did everything I could to get the book reviewed, gave copies away, ran ads, went to a local book club to share my book, networked with others, and did all sorts of crazy things (Remember the story I told earlier about sending a copy to an adult film actress, hoping she would talk kindly about the book on social media?) to get my book noticed.

But the most important marketing tactic that I didn't know was: Write the next book!

You would have thought I had learned my lesson after writing *Dorothea's Song*, but I didn't. I pushed hard on getting *Lost* reviewed and I wanted to see it shoot into the stratosphere. Keep in mind that back in 2011, there was still the awe around indie publishing with a few writers putting up a book and it selling tens of thousands of copies without any major marketing. I loved my book and believed it deserved a chance. I signed up for KDP select and ran promotions to give away copies of *Lost*, having the book rise in the rankings and hoping that more people would discover it once it cracked the top 150. With the first two years, I gave away more than 20,000 copies of *Lost*. I wanted it to be the book that made me become discovered, and I tried everything I could think of to "make it big."

But when I take an objective look back, I see there is a glaring question I refused to see back in 2011. Once I published *Lost* and spent time and money promoting it, what did I expect readers to buy next? Yes, I had my first book *Dorothea's Song* and my science fiction short story collection, but that was it.

I wasted a lot of time marketing a product that had nothing to come after it. Instead of wasting so much time, money, and energy on marketing *Lost*, I could have better spent that time by writing my next book and then the next and so on.

The best marketing tool I had at my disposal was to simply write another book in the series.

When a reader finished *Lost*, then she would see either in the front or back matter an ad for my next book. And at the end of book two, she would see an ad for book three. It took me a few years to learn all of this and how to effectively put together a strategy to build a reader base. And to be honest, I'm still working on executing that strategy.

Back in 2009, I wrote *Lost*, but I never allowed myself the creative freedom to think about what would happen after book one. I simply thought of a simple premise: "What happened to Cinderella after she married the prince?" I never did any brainstorming to come up with the answer to: "And then what?"

Thankfully, I didn't take decades to write *Stolen*. I published book two in 2012. That was as fast as I could write the book and have a full-time job. The key point for me was to focus on not giving up and finishing what I started. I needed time to plan out a story arc that encompassed twelve years in the time of my characters' lives. I wanted to think big, build a world that felt real, and write characters who I would be proud for my kids to read when they got older.

All of that took time and energy and not to mention a lot of effort.

Plan It Out

There is a big difference between wanting to write a book and choosing to build a media empire. Where you fall between those two choices will help dictate what you will want to learn and how to then execute your plan.

For example, if you have a book idea, I would recommend jotting down a few sentences about your idea. Take the opportunity to explore the idea a bit and take a step back and think big. Here's an example:

Let's go back in time and say that I'm thinking about writing my book *Lost*. Here's a general sketch of the plot.

Lost (book one)

What really happened after Cinderella married the prince? It's two years after the marriage, and Cinderella isn't happy. She's desperate to be rescued from her loveless marriage and writes to her faerie godmother, hoping her faerie godmother can save her. But when all she knows is turned upside down and the evil faerie, the Silver Fox, tries to possess her, Cinderella discovers a secret that shatters all she knows about who her mother was, and more importantly, who she is.

Stolen (book two)

Cinderella has moved to America to raise her daughter, but a witch hunter comes after her. She's been requested to come back to Europe to help England fight against Napoleon and the faerie queen. The stakes are raised and she refuses to come back until she realizes that refusing to help will destroy all she loves.

Found (book three)

Cinderella searches desperately for her kidnapped daughter. Napoleon has conquered all of Europe and now marches on Russia. Cinderella and her friends need to find a way to win the war, but more importantly, she wants to find her only child and save her.

In looking at the three short paragraphs, I've written enough ideas to tie together a story arc that will last through a trilogy and beyond. When I first wrote *Lost*, I never considered sequels. But from a marketing perspective, many readers like a series because they become invested in the characters and grow to love them over time. I had a perfect means of formulating a plan that would allow me to plan a series of books centered around Cinderella rather than just one book.

All of this is great, but again, what do you want to do with your writing career? Do you want to write one book? A trilogy? A huge Harry Potter–like series? Or do you want to write in multiple genres with more than a hundred books?

The road to being an author is so much more complicated than I originally thought, but that's good. I started my journey when I was nine years old with a simple idea: I wanted to entertain readers with my writing. And my personal goal was to escape from my own problems for a while in the worlds I made up. It was a win-win.

But over the years, I have expanded my original idea and started to plan out multiple series:

The Realms series

Dorothea's Song is the first book of a planned trilogy. Book two has been in draft form since 1999. Book three isn't written yet.

Cinderella's Secret Witch Diaries series

I have published three books and plan on a fourth (possibly a fifth and sixth).

A Witch's Coven series

Awakenings and *Betrayals* have been written. Book three is in the early planning stages.

The Jovian Gate Chronicles series

Faith was published in 2016, and I've plans for books two and three. I'm experimenting with this series because it's a crossover with *Cinderella's Secret Witch Diaries*—a major character from that series is front and center in this one.

Forthcoming projects

I wrote a new book in 2016 and planned it as a one-off. I have since written the first draft of that book, and it could be turned into a trilogy.

I look at this body of work like a proud father. I share this not to pat myself on the back but to share an extremely important point: I never thought I could create anything beyond *Dorothea's Song*. Now I have multiple series in production and only need to plan out what I want to write next. I have many options that compete for my time, and that's a good thing.

The only thing holding me back all these years was how I viewed myself. As soon as I stopped looking for validation from others and trusted in myself, ideas started locking into place. By setting a schedule, investing in myself (reading, learning, and practicing), and adding exercise into my life, I created a healthy life that fosters creativity.

Think big. Really big. I once heard Geoffrey M. Wahl, a prominent cancer researcher, say: "Shoot for the stars. If you only hit the moon, that's fine." With the books I have written and released to the world, I have print copies, ebook versions on multiple sales platform, and have Audible versions of the *Cinderella's Secret Witch Diaries* books. I have worked hard to diversify my writing portfolio in genre and format. I'm looking to continue to do that with book bundles, movie options, and virtual reality.

But none of this would have been possible if I didn't finish what I started!

Chapter 9: Create Your Business Plan

Build Your Plan

Now that you have had a chance to see where I'm coming from, talking about a business plan will make more sense. When I first started out, I only thought about writing a book. Even once I decided that I wanted to do a sequel to *Lost* and then book three, I truly didn't have a grasp of what my long-term plan would be. I was working full-time and juggled raising two kids. But I've had some time now to think and work on devising a plan.

When I first started out, I hadn't a clue. I had no idea what the hell I was doing except that I wanted to write stories. I made stuff up, enjoyed doing that, and wanted to find a way to share the stories with others. I only knew I wanted to write books, not how I would get there. I simply had no sense of how to turn my writing into a second career.

I'll be honest with you: I still don't have everything all figured out. Part of why I'm writing this book is because I want to explore a different style of writing. By going through the process of sharing what I think about writing, it's as though we're sitting down and having a conversation. Both of us get to benefit.

At this period in my life, I know that I like to write, want to hone my craft, keep putting out books, and to connect with like-minded authors, and most importantly, I want to connect with my readers. How I'm going to do all this has always been a bit sketchy. The good news though is that I've worked on putting together a plan and have built flexibility into it so that I can pivot as necessary.

I recommend taking stock of your business plan at least once a quarter through the calendar year. Every three months allows you time to get work done, assess where you are in the year, adjust course as necessary, and have the means to keep track of where you're headed.

The mind shift from "I want to write a book" to "I want to plan out my business" is a big shift and will take time.

What should be in your business plan?

Well, the U.S. Small Business Administration (SBA) has a nice website to teach you the basics.

https://www.sba.gov/starting-business/write-your-business-plan

The resources on the SBA website will give you enough to get started. I followed a similar outline for my business plan with some specifics that I found useful for me:

- What's my mission as an author?
- What are my products?
- What's the strategy behind my pricing?
- How will I fund my business?
- Over the next twenty-four months, what's my production schedule for books/audiobooks in the pipeline?
- Who am I trying to sell to?
- What's my marketing plan?
- Where do I see the business going in the next 5 years?

Yes, there are a lot of questions listed there, but they'll help ground and empower you to take your business seriously. Again, when we're talking about finishing what you started, only you can decide whether you want to write one book and then quit or if you want to write many books. If you choose to create many, then you'll want a plan. I know some of you might be freaking out because putting a commitment to a plan might seem difficult. I get that. I resisted creating a business plan for years because I thought I would simply write the great American (or insert country of your choice here) novel and all the marketing would just be handled by some publishing company.

When reality starts knocking on your door and you realize you're not swimming in money and just worked your tail off, then your choice is clear. Are you going to toss in the towel and give up or keep trying by working smarter?

Quitting doesn't mean you're a failure; it simply means you've decided to pursue different goals. If my book helps you to realize that the writing life isn't for you, then better that you know that now than to slog along for years, not take joy in your work, and slowly fall off with writing until the dream becomes a husk of the vibrant cornucopia that it once was.

If you choose to go on or happen to strike it big with one of your first books, you're going to want a business plan so you can have a foundation on which to build.

Mission Statement

When writing the mission statement, describe your business and what you're trying to accomplish. In my business plan, I wrote about the type of products I produce (print books, ebooks, blog posts, articles, and audio books) and why I write. Here's a bit from my mission statement:

"I will continue to build my brand (identifying with people who feel lost and broken from dysfunctional families, showing the way forward on how I continue to work on bettering myself and find healing and connection) and the novels that I write."

My business plan is for me. It's a personal document poured my heart and soul into, giving me a time capsule so I can see what I thought and felt back when I wrote it. And the beauty of a business plan is that it's a living and breathing document. I can tweak it as necessary. Look at Apple or Microsoft. How have their businesses dramatically changed over the decades? They've embraced technological changes, and as indie authors, so will we.

List Your Products

In this section of my business plan, I listed all my books, when they were published, links to all the places they are available (Kobo, iBooks, Amazon, Nook Press, etc.) and which format (print, ebook, audiobook) they are available.

Pricing

I researched all the top sellers on Amazon and listed the prices I found for ebooks and then listed my current prices. I also listed the print prices as well.

After reviewing what the trends were in the ebook industry, I matched according to that and also listed some thoughts for the next year. I did this on purpose so that when I came back to review my plan,

I had the opportunity to adjust my pricing or stay the course, depending on what the market trends were in the present (or what was being forecast in the near future).

Funding

I went through the laborious task of writing down all my books that I had published and listed all the sales I had, broken down by product type, from 2011 to 2016. At that time, I had published the following books:

Lost
Stolen
Found
Cinderella's Secret Witch Diaries: Books 1 - 3 (ebook bundle)
Dorothea's Song
Awakenings
Betrayals
Jovian Gate Chronicles: Short Story Collection

I analyzed the sales by print, audiobook (where available), and ebook. The work involved pulling all my old sales spreadsheets together which is something I'd rather not have to do again, but it gives me great insight into my sales. For example, I now know that 75.6% of the sales for *Lost* (book one in my *Cinderella's Secret Witch Diaries* series) is in digital. I did not count any free books given away as part of a KDP select or permafree. I only counted actual sales that people spent their hard-earned money on to buy my books.

After I finished tallying up all the data, I had an extremely clear picture. I took my emotions and put it aside, looking at the raw numbers. My book *Lost* has sold the best and books two and three of the series are similarly placed in the number two and three slots.

I now have a picture of what is working and what isn't. Granted, I have not promoted *The Realms* or *The Witch's Coven* series as much as *Cinderella's Secret Witch Diaries*, but it does give me pause to think about what my next book will be. I can write book four in the *Cinderella's Secret Witch Diaries* series (where I have a small following) or finish up one of the other series.

What I like about the business plan is that I've tied real data into it so that I can use it as a means of moving forward and helping me make business decisions. One decision might be about the book I wrote in 2016 that's not part of a series. Sure, I'd like to release it in 2017, but it might be hard to market because I don't have a built-in reader base for it. I would need to work on a marketing plan that would take that into consideration.

But what about you? Some of you who are reading this book might only have an idea of writing your first book. Maybe you're first starting out and my listing my books down and talking about sales, strategy, and several years of planning your strategy out is intimidating. I get that. I do.

Let me ask you this: If you are feeling overwhelmed, why not break down the pieces of the business plan and stretch the work out over time? Chunk it out. It's the same idea as writing a book. Remember, we're in this marathon together. A business plan does not need to be finished in a week. It took me five years and having written a bunch of books before I even did mine!

If you're not finished your first book yet, just think how much easier it is to get that first draft down. Start small and when you think about products or how you will fund the business, be honest with yourself. How much do you expect to sell? And what type of books (print, ebooks, and audiobooks)? Just write down what you would like to do for that first book of yours and you'll have a baseline that can be adapted over time.

Now that you have a list of what you want, I also recommend writing down how much money you'll need to publish your book. Here is a list of my expenses for 2016:

2016 Expenses

- Google Apps for business ($50/year)
- Squarespace website/hosting ($192/year)
- Facebook Ads ($275.38)
- Book promotions ($381)
- Faith cover design and web banner ($500)
- Proofreading fee for Faith ($235)
- Web domain and proxy registration fees ($22.42/year)
- Copyright registration fees ($35)
- Mailchimp ($390)
- Instafreebie (October - December) ($60)

Total 2016 Business Expenses: $2140.80

For first-time writers, let me break the expenses down for you:

I opted to create a website to market my work (using Squarespace.com) and bought the domain name (ronvitale.com). I use Mailchimp to send out my email newsletters and manage my subscriber list and tie Instafreebie into Mailchimp to obtain more subscribers, and the rest of my expenses are for book cover designs, professional proofreading, and advertising.

It adds up, doesn't it?

The one bit of advice that I would put out there for any writer is to spend the money on hiring the best editor you can possibly afford and a great cover. The higher the quality of your book, the more enticing your book will be for readers.

Is it possible to publish a book cheaper than the fees I listed here? Of course. You could always run a different type of website on Wordpress.com and save money there, but I've found that it's a lot easier for me to spend some money on a solid website so that I don't have to worry about maintenance, uptime, and other technical issues.

I've seen cover sales go for a lot cheaper than the 99designs.com that I've used over the last two years, but I've never been impressed with twenty-five-dollar covers. Often the inexpensive covers look just like that—cheap, bad photoshopping, and it shows. When your cover is sometimes the first touchpoint with a potential reader, I want to make certain that my covers grab you and pull you in.

If you look back at my covers from 2011-2014 for *Lost, Stolen,* and *Found* from the *Cinderella's Secret Witch Diaries Series,* you'll see some of the challenges that I encountered and growing pains. I opted for inexpensive covers. The graphic designer I worked with did a great job, but I lacked the skill to give her the direction she needed. The fonts are difficult to read and the pictures for books two and three do not effectively communicate the story to the reader. I'm currently in the process of having my *Cinderella's Secret Witch Diaries* covers revamped.

My books from 2015 up to the present were created by two different designers through 99designs, and the quality is much better, but the costs were higher.

I've worked hard on writing the best books I can, having them be as error free as possible with strong covers. The reason is that these works of mine will represent me in online bookstores throughout the world—for years to come. The investment I have made is steep, but I am choosing to learn from the mistakes I made on my first few books.

The good news, hopefully, is that if you are also working full-time, you will have some income to allocate to your writing business. You'll need a computer, internet access, and some of the services that I listed above (website host, email list management, domain name for your website, covers, proofreading, etc.).

Production Schedule

Once you've thought through your finances, you can then sit down and plan out your production schedule for the next twenty-four months. If you're a first-time writer, putting down dates on a calendar might be hard to do because you've not experienced what it will really take for you to write a book.

It took me eighteen months to write, rewrite, edit, format, and publish *Lost*. Four years later, I pumped out *Awakenings* in five months (one month to write the first draft and the remaining four months for rewriting, cover design, proofreading, formatting, and then launching). There are fellow indie authors who can knock a book out in a month. Some write twenty books a year. I worked full-time, wrote two books in a year, and nearly imploded with the amount of work.

Here's the thing: You can worry about the work and not know how much it will take you to write a book or you can sit down and just do it. When writing up your business plan, do your best and estimate. After you've written your third or fourth book, you'll have a much better handle on what the actual timeframe will be for you.

I know that over the years I have beaten myself up and wondered why I couldn't just sit down and knock out four books a year. Of course, I could make this happen if I wanted, but I would have to sacrifice too much in my life. I would never get back the times that I could have spent with my kids—changing their diapers, teaching them how to throw a ball, and running up to them and tickling them. I opted to focus on my family.

For me, the reality is that my full-time job pays the bills. When I factor out the time I work and the commute time to my house, I'm spending, on average, eleven to twelve hours of my day at my day job. Factor in sleep, chores (cleaning up from dinner, wash, etc.) and there's a tiny amount of time left to spend with my family. After all of that, I then choose to write.

Sure, I could switch things around and sleep even less or spend less time reading or exercising, but I've worked hard on finding a healthy balance for me. What that balance is for you will be different. The purpose of writing the production schedule down for the next twenty-four months is to have you focus on your longer-term plan and get you to stick to it.

Intimidated by a twenty-four-month plan? Then start with twelve months. Write down the estimated amount of time you expect to need to write a book. A good way to estimate is to track your daily word count over the course of a month and multiply that out until you hit your word count (65,000 words? 85,000?).

Remember, don't beat yourself up. Overestimate the time you need if you're a first-time novelist. You can always revise your production schedule later.

Target Market

I liked writing this part of the business plan because it forced me to think of my ideal reader. I paired up what I thought with data I received from Google Analytics, and this helped me develop a plan for my readers.

The traffic on my website is almost seventy percent female, and that matches nicely to what I had in mind with my books. However, what I had not expected is that my audience skews older than I originally anticipated. I had thought my readers would fall within the ages of nineteen to twenty-seven. But from receiving email from my readers and combining that with my Google Analytics data, I can extrapolate that my readers are in an older demographic.

In the beginning, you might not have much data to pull from, but you can garner information from your website's analytics and even put together surveys to your mailing list. All of this takes time and effort, but it's worth thinking about in the long run. When you write, having the readers in mind is often helpful to me.

Write down who you think your target market is, and tweak this as you learn more.

Marketing Plan

If you're writing your first book, I would highly recommend focusing on writing book two as your main marketing goal. Once you have your first book out, you'll want to have readers buy it, but they'll then want to see what other books you have.

I wasted too much time focusing on marketing book one of my series. Way too much time. I look back and admit that I could have saved months of time by just writing book two directly after I published book one.

How you choose to plan the rollout of your books can make all the difference. Some authors write three books and then release them through the course of the year. I couldn't do that because I wasn't patient enough. I needed to get my book out as fast as I could. Since *Lost* took me eighteen months to write and publish, I didn't want to sit on it for the two years that it would take me to write books two and three. However, if you're a fast writer, maybe writing three books in a series and then releasing them close together is the way to go.

There is no right or wrong way to move forward. The only issue that I would say is: If you don't write any other books, you'll not have any other product to sell. Readers, at least in this first part of the twenty-first century, like series.

After you decide what your production schedule will be, there are many choices for marketing. You can try to score a Bookbub ad, run Facebook ads, buy space in smaller book newsletters that send out their emails to tens of thousands of people—the choice is yours.

There are some ads that work well and others that don't. Instead of getting into the gritty details on advertising, I like to pull back and think of a strategy first.

I believe that building up an email list is the next most important thing I can do to help build out my marketing strategy. Once I had readers to market to, that made all the difference. I wish I would have started earlier on building my subscriber base because I then focused on automation emails and could naturally, through the course of several months, ask readers to buy the next book in the series or ask them to leave a review for my book and also offer them free books/stories.

My marketing strategy is focused on building my relationship with my readers.

There are more ways to advertise than you'll have money, but for your marketing strategy, what will you choose to roll out?

I believe in focusing on readers, finding where those readers are, and engaging with them. The actual execution (advertising plan) can take on many permutations, but I believe it's integral to have a marketing approach first, and then think through the tactical aspects.

For example, if you know who your target audience is, then I would recommend you test those assumptions and work on then building out a plan you can execute over time.

The strategy: Are you using Facebook, Twitter, Goodreads, and other platforms to drive traffic to subscribe to your email list? Or do you have another strategy in mind?

What I have decided to do is to focus on providing the most authentic outreach I can to my readers. Either they'll like that and subscribe to my list or they won't. Since I want to build a relationship with my readers over time and offer them incentives and connect with them, my marketing strategy is currently focused on building my email list. Since I then would have control of the emails in the list, I have the ability to then create campaigns, devise an editorial calendar on the type of communications to send out to the list, and then use my limited funds on advertising that will continually drive traffic to my email signup page rather than just coldly asking people I don't know (and who don't know me) to go buy one of my books.

The landing pages I have created on my website help me build my audience, increase my reach with actual readers, and funnel those individuals into my carefully planned out content strategy. I can then continue to engage with my readers on a regular basis.

As part of my marketing strategy, I have run ads on various services that promote indie authors to their readers via an electronic newsletter, I've taken part in reciprocal blog posts with fellow authors, and I have run Facebook ads, driving traffic to my email signup page. The strategy is simple: I offer book one for free if a person signs up to my email list.

Over the last fifteen months, I've aligned my marketing goals and pivoted from trying to directly get strangers to buy my book to giving new subscribers a free book and then building a relationship with them so that these people will then purchase books two and three in my *Cinderella's Secret Witch Diaries* series.

I've made that change on purpose because it's extremely difficult to sell something to a person who doesn't know who I am and has no context to what I stand for and represent in my writing. Giving away book one and then showing new subscribers, via emails that they then receive over the next six weeks after subscribing, why they would want to buy my books because they know what themes I write about has helped me sell more books.

In the past, I tried to simply sell via ads and had hardly any success.

What your marketing strategy will be can be any number of outcomes. There are many other books out there to talk through various approaches with you, but I wanted to get the basics down. For me, authors need to connect with readers. Find out how to do that with your target readers, do it often, and build that list up!

Future Casting

The last part of the business plan is to think about where you see your business in the next five years. If you're just starting out, yes, this might be a challenge—especially if you haven't completed a book yet. But think big here. Do you want to finish several trilogies in that time frame? Or are you looking to morph into a publishing house where you publish other people's books under your imprint?

My own personal goals have evolved and matured over time. Initially, I simply wanted to finish my first book. I wanted people to buy it and for the book to be successful. I didn't understand that I not only needed to know how to write, and to become better at that, but I needed to understand marketing, social media tools, search engine optimization, formatting my manuscripts into ebooks and email marketing. I went from wanting to publish one book to dreaming bigger. I want to publish many books through different series and to have these books be available in different product forms (audio book, print, ebook) and am open to my books being optioned for movies and even as stories via virtual reality or games.

In the non-fiction realm, I wish to write books to help teach people how to be a successful indie author, but I also wish to be a speaker at conferences. My ultimate plan is to create a media empire (I know, that's a strong phrase there.) in which I license my intellectual property to various companies and teach others how to do the same.

All of those dreams started by my simply wanting to write a book. Now that I have been working on publishing books for more than five years, I have expanded my dreams as I've conquered my original ones. I don't wish to stop being a writer, but I want to become better at it and to find more exciting and authentic ways of connecting with readers.

Just because you set your goals down for the next five years doesn't mean they're written in stone. No, that's not the case! But if you shoot for the stars, then you have a chance to reflect along the way on how you want to move forward with your writing career. What you want today probably will change over time and that's fine.

But if you're not taking the time to think, and to write down what you want, you might be missing an opportunity to truly get in touch with your inner self. Why are you up early in the morning or staying up late to write? Why are you choosing to do this? What is your ultimate goal?

My goal is simple: I want to connect with other people and not only entertain readers with my books but to have them identify with my characters, knowing they can see themselves, at times, in them.

No one is forcing you to write. It's going to be hard work and will take a lot of time and energy. Many writers fail, stop writing, drop out, and give up on their dreams. What is going to make you not do that, and where do you see yourself five years from now?

I'll end this chapter with reminding you to finish what you start. Whatever that means to you, take stock in not just the short-term goal of wanting to write a book, but take a high-level approach and allow your dreams to be put to paper. When you are tired and writing at 5:00 a.m. before work, I would recommend that you hang up your goals somewhere so you can see them. Some of you will be motivated by money, fame, prestige, and others will have different driving forces and goals.

For me, yes, money would be nice, but achieving more financial success isn't going to motivate me enough when I'm tired and need to finish a book in the wee hours of the morning. About a year and a half ago, I received an email from a reader who has multiple sclerosis (MS). She thanked me for writing the *Cinderella's Secret Witch Diaries* books and asked if she could receive a free audiobook of *Lost*. I was running a promotion at the time, and she wanted to know if she had responded early enough to get one of the free coupon codes. She also wanted to know if she could receive autographed copies of my books, having purchased them recently.

She went on to explain how much she loved my books but had severe complications due to the disease, often having intense migraines, and had trouble reading. She explained to me that being able to listen to a book helped her immensely. I sent her the free coupon code to the audiobook she had requested and also sent her three autographed books from the series. When she received the package in the mail, she wrote me the nicest letter of thanks back. Although I had only done such a small thing for her, she was so happy that I not only had given her the free audiobook but also the autographed copies.

And that's why I write. I get up and work before the sun rises because I know there are readers out there who love my books. For me, it's all about my readers. Knowing how much that woman loved my books and how they helped her through her rough days helped me realize that I am, in a small way, making a difference to people in the world. That's why I push myself so hard to write. Knowing that I can help people is a big motivator for me. What's your motivation and where do you see yourself in five years with your writing? Think about that and write it down in your business plan.

Chapter 10: Launch Your Book

After all the hard work, the day has finally come. Your book is ready to see the light of day and be released to the world. If you're a first-time author and it's your first book, you'll have some decisions to make.

- Do you want the book to go wide or be available only on Amazon?
- Did you want to have the book available for pre-order?
- What's your launch strategy?
- Do you have a clear call to action in the front and back matter of the book?
- What's your social plan?
- What is your plan to obtain reviews for the book?
- Do you want to buy ads to promote the book?

I've mentioned this before, but it's worth saying again. If I could go back in time, I would have saved myself a lot of frenetic energy and pulled back on the marketing to focus instead on writing book two. When I look at the list of questions above, there are a lot of decisions (and work) that are tied into a book launch. There's a whole science to it.

Going Wide

Many indie authors debate this point, and there isn't one right answer about how to release your books. To compromise, I often choose to launch the book exclusively to Amazon for the first ninety days by being signed up to Amazon's Kindle Direct Publishing Select, and then at the end of ninety days, I opt out and then offer my book to Nook Press, iBooks (using Draft2Digital), and Kobo.

For me, the reality is that my sales are mostly on Amazon. For other authors, that's not the case. Yes, Kindle Unlimited is available once you're signed up for KDP Select, and that could earn you some money through Kindle Edition Normalized Pages (KENP). For KENP, Amazon tracks the number of pages read, and that's how you're paid. Readers sign up for Kindle Unlimited for $9.99 a month and then can read, for free, books that are in KDP Select. The KENP number is then calculated on a per page basis. This translates (at the time of this writing) to around $0.0058 per page. For my book *Faith* (that I currently have in KDP Select), if a reader finishes the entire book, then I earn $1.65.

285 pages * $0.0058 per page = $1.65

I have my book priced at $2.99 on Amazon, but readers who have Kindle Unlimited can read as much of the book as they want, and I am only paid for what they read. Let's discuss that for a moment.

When I used to buy a hardback book, I'd spend twenty-four dollars, and I'd bring it home and read it cover to cover. There was an inherent worth attached to the book. I spent a good amount of money on the book and wanted to make sure that I squeezed every ounce of entertainment I could out of it. Once I finished the book, I'd then lend it to a friend.

But the books I borrowed from the library didn't have the same worth attached to it. I recently took a book out of a library, started to read it, didn't like it (which hardly happens for me), and took it back without finishing it. I felt guilty for not reading the book because I'm an author and like to give a fellow writer the benefit of the doubt, but I just couldn't get into the book. I was bored. I took the book back and that was that.

Now imagine if I had Kindle Unlimited. I could start reading up to ten books (that are in KDP Select) at the same time, and authors are only paid for what I read. Because the intrinsic value of the book is skewed into the "all you can eat" model, readers are choosing to be pickier about what they actually read. Additionally, an ebook is one of many digital items on your smartphone or Kindle, and there isn't the same sense of physical space taken up by the book. I leave my physical books by my bedside. I can see the covers, and they're a reminder of what my "to read" list looks like. On my Kindle, I often forget to go back to my library and see what I have available. I have received books as gifts, and they're lost in my digital library because of all the books I can now easily place on my phone. (Do you hear me Amazon? I'd love to be able to select the home screen of my Kindle to display what I'm currently reading. That would be really nice.)

There's an ongoing debate on whether KDP Select is helpful or hurtful to authors. On one hand, KDP select used to be a great way to promote your book. Back in 2009, an author could offer her book for free for up to five days and have thousands of readers download her book. A percentage of those readers would then choose to buy the next book in the series.

But over the last eight years, readers are being trained that music, movies, and books are not as intrinsically valuable as they used to be. With streaming services, why buy a movie if Netflix offers it? Same is true with music. I have Spotify now with 20,000,000 songs. Why do I need to buy a CD? I'm spending fifteen dollars a month on a family plan. But the reality is that the musicians are not seeing a large paycheck from streaming music services. With Amazon's KENP, authors see only $0.0058 per page read. If a reader picks up a book and only reads a third of it, then that's all an author is paid. Whereas, if a reader buys my book for $2.99, I earn $2.05—no matter if the reader does or doesn't read the book.

The publishing world has been turned upside down by Amazon's new business model, and I fully expect more changes to come. The big publishing houses are resisting joining in Kindle Unlimited because there aren't as much profits in their joining. For readers, Kindle Unlimited can be a good deal. Amazon makes business decisions that are best for them and their customers—not for authors. Remember that.

With that being true, I've had to make some hard choices. When I first started out, I only had my books on Amazon, but I began seeing more and more authors choosing to go wide and distribute their work with other online sellers. Why? With any investment, I believe that diversification is the wisest course of action. If Amazon chooses to lower the royalty rate drastically and I only had my books in their platform, I would be adversely affected. When I choose to sign up for KDP Select, I'm agreeing that my book cannot be sold anywhere for those ninety days except on Amazon.

Now do you see why this can be a difficult choice?

To compromise, I experiment by offering my book exclusively to Amazon for the first ninety days and then going wide after that. If Amazon were to change royalty rates or go out of business, my books would still be on sale in other platforms.

I like having a diversified portfolio. But the reality is that most of my sales are still coming from Amazon. That's not true of all indie authors as I have networked with other writers who do extremely well on Kobo or iBooks.

Still, if this is your first book, you'll need to make a decision. What will work best for you? Talk with other writers, do your research on KDP Select, and then make an informed decision.

Pre-orders

Setting up a pre-order makes sense, but you will need to plan a strategy around it. For example, if you do not have an email list or a way to advertise your book being available in advance, then you're probably not going to set this up.

On Amazon, there are specific rules you will need to follow, and if you do not follow those rules, then you risk the chance of being banned from ever having a pre-order setup on Amazon again. How do I know this? I had this happen to me.

I tried my first pre-order back in 2015 and made a mistake in the release date. If you do not provide the final manuscript by three days before the launch date, you'll run into trouble. The problem I had is that I misunderstood how the dates were set for the pre-order and I selected them wrong.

When I discovered what I had done, I wrote to Amazon's customer service and immediately begged forgiveness for the mistake I had made. All turned out fine, but the experience did stress me out, and I did not like having such a hard deadline hanging over me. Maybe if I had already finished the book and was sitting on the final version, I would have felt differently, but working full-time and unannounced day job deadlines cropping up took time out of my rewriting and formatting schedule.

For me, with all the stresses of my full-time job, I have decided to hold off and not offer pre-orders at this time. If you choose to, be sure to do your research because Amazon recently changed the policy on pre-orders.

Launch Strategy

Speaking of strategy, what is the plan? Beg all your friends and family members to buy your book? Don't laugh. Many first-time authors try that approach because they focused on the writing of the book but not the marketing. When I look back at how I launched *Lost*, I cringe now.

I had no email subscriber list, advertising budget, or built-in reviewer base and no sequel on the horizon. I published *Lost* on Amazon in KDP Select and offered it for free. To date, I have given more than 40,000 copies of *Lost* away over the last six years. That's great, but is it really?

What did I really think would happen once people downloaded my book? You can laugh at me, it's okay. I share my story with you because you can learn from my mistakes and not duplicate them. Here's my thought process at the time:

I wrote *Dorothea's Song* many years ago and now have it on Amazon. I'll release *Lost,* use the five free days of giving it away on Amazon through KDP Select, and hope that people will then buy *Dorothea's Song.* Did my plan work? Nope.

Why? Because I had not put much thought (okay, any) into the strategy behind my book launch. I simply wanted to write the book and release it to the wild, and then the magical gold rush of KDP Select would snatch me up and bring me on a magic carpet ride. My launch strategy failed miserably because I had written a fantasy book for teen girls and was then asking them to buy *Dorothea's Song* which was an epic fantasy geared for boys. The crossover between the two audiences is almost nil.

Once I realized I couldn't sell *Dorothea's Song* to readers of *Lost,* I focused on asking book reviewers to leave a review on Amazon or to publish a review on their blog. I started to shift my strategy from begging friends and family to buy/read my book to have respected book reviewers share my book to their blog readers. I needed to find readers, but I didn't have a lot of concrete tactics to implement my strategy.

Now I have a different plan:

- Tease the cover out months in advance to my subscribers.
- About six weeks out, ask a segment of my subscriber base if they wish to receive a free Advance Reader Copy (ARC) and agree to leave a review on Amazon.
- Ask book reviewers to accept an ARC and post a review on their blog.
- Network with like-minded authors to help promote each other's new books on launch day.

- Post the release of the book on social media (Twitter, Facebook, etc.) on launch day.
- Share on Kindleboards.com and other similar sites (Facebook and Goodreads groups).
- Run any advertising on Facebook, driving traffic to the first book in the series.
- Change all my call to actions in relevant books to advertise that the new book is now available.
- On launch day, share the news of a sale with my subscribers.

The overall strategy is to find a way to have my book be found by new readers but also by the right readers. Chris Fox goes into detail on this in his book *Six Figure Author*. His premise is pretty simple: Amazon's algorithms will kick in and promote your book to readers if you're selling copies to your core audience. If you write historical fantasies and within the first two weeks sell a select number of books to readers who typically buy those type of books, Amazon's algorithms will kick in and suggest your book to other readers who also buy historical fantasies. Why? Amazon wants to make more money, and they can do so by using the data they have on customers and matching new products with their customer base. Want to learn more about this, then check out Chris' book.

In getting back to launching your book, I've used the tactics listed above to promote my book, and I'm continuing to learn and try new things. There are many, many more ways to promote a book launch, but for me, what I've listed above is a good start.

You can give away an Amazon gift card to a random reader who leaves a review on Amazon or send people a signed copy of your book. You can come up with social media ideas and read a section of your book to a live Google Hangouts or try Facebook live streaming—the ideas are endless.

At the end of the day, you will need to come up with a plan on what to do and when (and how). When I first started out on my journey as an indie author, I embraced the freedom that I had in not having to work within the confines of a traditional publishing contract. However, I also learned that I was now responsible for not just the writing of the book but its production, release, and promotion.

In retrospect, I had no clue what I was getting myself into and admit that I have a lot yet to learn because the publishing industry continues to change so dramatically. Seven years ago, an author could release a book on Amazon KDP Select and become rich. Today you'll need to be much more thorough and strategic in planning your release and thinking about the long term of your career.

Call to Action (CTA)

Calls to action are a simple and effective way of having your additional products put in front of readers. Over the last few years, there has been much debate on where to put the CTAs, but here's what I have decided to do:

If I'm writing a series and am releasing book three, then I go back and reformat book two. In the front and back of the ebook version of book two, I put the cover for book three and a simple blurb to excite the reader that a new book is available. But the most important thing: I add a link to a web page.

My intention is simple: A reader downloads my book on her phone and sees the cover for book three and a link. If she ignores that call to action, then she finishes the book and again sees the cover for book three and a link to buy the book. My link might be: "Buy book three now!" or something that's catchy.

Tip: Do not put direct "Buy now" links to Amazon in the Kindle version of your ebook unless you use a URL shortener.

Why? I learned the hard way that Apple and Amazon do not play well together. Since I'm a reader as well as an author, I always like to jump into my reader mode, buy my own book, load it on my iPhone, and check the book out. (I go through an extensive testing phase before launch—I email the .mobi file to my Kindle Reader app on my iPhone as well and go through every single page.) When testing my books out, I discovered that Apple does not allow a link from within the Kindle Reader app to go directly to Amazon.com. Yep, you heard that right. At the time I am writing this, you can't buy a book through the Kindle Reader app's browser on your iPhone. Apple has the iBook store, and they're looking for a piece of the action.

For a while, I had individualized .mobi and .epub files depending on the various platforms, but that quickly became a nightmare to update my CTAs in all my books. Each time I released a new book, I'd have to go back and upload several new files. I wasted a lot of formatting and testing time, getting all my books to work right.

Now that I use Squarespace for my web hosting, I built out a landing page for all of my books. On my landing page, I can list the cover, short description, and then links to where a reader can buy all the various versions of my book. Another option would be to use Draft2Digital's universal book links. You can create a nice landing page that lists all the versions of your books so that readers can then buy whatever they want.

If you're writing your first book and are thinking of bagging the CTA idea, please don't! If you can't advertise book two of a series, then why not offer a free story for those readers who sign up for your mailing list? It's a great way to connect with your readers.

Keep in mind: Once you set up an opt-in mailing list page, you'll need to create a landing page that showcases the offer and collects the person's email and then have a content strategy in place. I would advise not to simply collect a reader's email and then forget about it. How would you feel if you signed up for an email list but didn't hear anything from the author for months?

I like to think of subscribers as cultivating friends. I need to spend time reaching out to friends, share stories with them, have a laugh, maybe share some fun pictures. For me, I like to write about my areas of interest and also share promotions from other indie authors with my subscribers. The power of the beginning and end of an ebook is not to be forgotten. I recommend that you use that space wisely.

Not sure what to put in the front and back of your ebook? Download one of my books at smurturl.it/xt9aeh or another indie author's and study what we've done.

Social Media

There are many social media platforms, and depending on your target audience, certain tools are more effective for you than others. Back in 2008 when I joined Twitter, I saw a world of possibilities and a means to communicate. I took the opportunity to learn Twitter and Facebook and created channels for the company I worked for at the time. But I also learned that social media isn't the place to necessarily sell your products to people.

I like to think of it this way: In real life, if I were to go to a large picnic in the park, I would see lots of different tables with different families and friends eating, talking, and playing games. One of my social media ads might read, "For a limited time, *Cinderella's Secret Witch*

Diaries on sale for $0.99. #Kindle #Indie." If I were to walk up to a table and say that, the people at that table would either think I was crazy or ignore me.

I have used social media to build relationships and engage people. I do not see the various social media platforms as a means to sell directly to customers (Facebook ads excluded). I'm not saying that you can't sell using social media tools, but I've followed enough indie authors over the years that I've had to stop reading their tweets. Most of the content that the authors were sharing out was simply advertising copy. Buy this, get this, do this now!

Social media can be so much more than that. The challenge, as with everything in an indie author career, is time. Many might tell you that you need to be on Pinterest, Instagram, Facebook, and Twitter. You need to live stream content and have a YouTube channel and a website and a pony so that you can give your readers a pony ride!

Again, it's not possible to do it all.

If you're a best-selling author and you're bringing in enough money to support yourself and you have a budget to hire a virtual assistant, yes, then invest in having someone help you with the platforms. Over the last eight years that I've been on Twitter, I've seen author after author fade away from the platform.

Recently, I had to make a choice and it was a difficult one. I could be on social media or I could write my books. The time that I used to be on Twitter, I now use for writing, reading (which is so important as a writer), and learning (reading blog posts and taking part in webinars to teach me marketing). As much as I like Twitter, I needed to disengage to make more time for myself. I have too many other tasks to complete in a day.

I want to be careful with what I'm saying: I do believe it's important to have a Facebook author page as well as a Twitter account. If your writing would be directly enhanced by using Pinterest or Instagram, then I would recommend being active on those platforms. For example, if you write cookbooks or write about clothing or jewelry, then I would highly recommend building a platform on Pinterest or Instagram. Not necessarily to sell, but to build an audience. Connect and engage with like-minded people, and then when it's time to market your book, you would have a select group of people who would be interested in what you have to sell.

From 2008 to 2012, I used Twitter much differently than I do today. Today I am on Twitter to get a pulse into what the world is interested in. I also like using Twitter to network with other authors. If you're writing your first book, I would recommend creating a Twitter account, branding it as the voice you want to portray with the themes that you write about, and have some catching graphics for your profile page.

Then simply tweet from time to time about the type of things you enjoy. Be authentic on the platform rather than a bot, trying to sell your books everywhere you go. I follow fellow authors and use Twitter's list functionality to build a community of authors that I follow on a regular basis.

I then use Hootsuite to create streams so that I can set up channels for the various Twitter lists I have. If you're not familiar with Twitter or Hootsuite, setting up the lists and streams is simple.

You can follow these simple steps:

Visit the Twitter page of the person/organization you would like to add to a list on Twitter. Click on the gears icon, select "Add or remove from lists…"

Then on the next page, include the person in the list you want or create a new list. You'll then need to decide if you would like the list to be public (for all Twitter users to see) or private.

I've always thought Twitter has done a poor job in promoting their features and what you can do with the tool. Twitter isn't a platform that's easy to grasp when compared to Instagram. Unfortunately, the user interface on Twitter can be challenging if you don't know all the features.

Once you have a list created, let's say "indie authors," simply do some Google searches, find the authors you would like to follow on Twitter, and then add them to your list. The possibilities are endless. You can use Twitter for competitive research, following all the publishers, agents or traditional authors, learning what they tweet about, the articles they share, and a whole host of other great information.

Now that you have your list created on Twitter, create a stream in Hootsuite by associating your Twitter account with Hootsuite.com. Add a stream in Hootsuite, select Twitter and then your username profile, and chose the list you'd like to add as a stream. Now be sure to have the Hootsuite app on your phone, and the next time you're stuck in line at the supermarket, you can pull up Hootsuite and look through all your lists. It's easy.

But the true power of Twitter, in my humble opinion, is in its ability to level the playing field. If I want to send a tweet to Neil Gaiman, I can do so, and he's been extremely active on Twitter, responding to people. Of course, whether someone is or isn't active on Twitter is an obvious blocking factor, but you can congratulate someone, offer help, or provide value to people in many ways. Over the years, I have written articles on my blog and then shared the piece with like-minded authors, knowing they were working on similar topics in the publishing field. That connection has helped me form bonds with the indie author community and even helped land me interview spots for several podcasts.

The possibilities are endless. Keep in mind that I am not currently using Twitter as a means to sell my books to readers. Twitter has changed dramatically in the last two years, and I'm seeing more people in publishing talking rather than readers wanting to buy books. I know that Twitter can be a powerful advertising tool, but I have chosen not to spend my limited budget on the platform. One effective means of advertising on Twitter would be to take your email list, export it and upload it to Twitter, and then pay for ads to target your subscribers.

If your subscribers do not see your email and open it to learn of the special offer you're providing for a book sale, then you have an opportunity to catch their eye on Twitter or Facebook.

For advertising my books, I've had more success with Facebook, but it's also expensive. Over time, Facebook has changed their algorithms so that your post is only being organically seen by a small percentage of those individuals who have liked the page. Why? Well, it's simple. Facebook wants you to "boost" your posts so that they can ensure that your article shows up in your fans' newsfeed. I have experimented with boosting posts but prefer running Facebook ads because in the ad manager I can target the demographic I want. That's the true power behind Facebook advertising.

This book isn't meant to go into the specifics of setting up a Facebook campaign, but I will share with you the basics. Essentially, you'll need to create a graphic (There are specific sizes and restrictions on the amount of text Facebook will allow you to have on the image.) and provide a small amount of text.

After you select who you would like to serve the ad to (male/female, age category, areas of interest, geographic location, etc.), you'll also need to decide how much you want to spend each day on the ad. I've experimented with five dollars per day and targeted women who like books similar to mine. Over the course of my campaign, my Facebook ad would show in people's feeds, and those individuals would click and opt in to my email subscriber list. There is a whole science to Facebook ads and how effective they can be, but again, there are only twenty-four hours in a day. What are your priorities?

If I were to spend hours a day on Twitter and Facebook, that's less time I have spending time with my family, writing, reading and learning more about marketing.

For me, the math was simple:

Work: 11 hours
Sleep: 6.5 hours
Dinner/family time: 2 hours

The 4.5 hours I have left each day is split between paying bills, exercising, writing, reading, watching TV, reading blog posts, oh, and spending time with my wife.

Even one hour spent on Facebook and Twitter each day eats too much of my personal time. Campaigns take time to set up in Facebook. Creating the ads, writing the copy, doing A/B testing, etc. It's not easy.

I have decided to test the waters from time to time in order to learn how to run Facebook ads, and I go on Twitter less and less these days because I have found more value in connecting with authors on private Facebook groups. Instead of barraging readers with "Buy NOW!!" ads and tweets, I opted at an early stage to share articles on my Facebook page, showing the things that I like. I want people to know more about me and what I stand for, and I show, by example, what I'm interested in as a person. My time on social media is to be authentic and helpful and not a spambot.

If you're starting out and you're working full-time, what will work for you? Yes, I believe setting up Twitter and Facebook are important to showcase pictures of your books and have your biography and links to your website out there, but I would not recommend tweeting up a storm if you're working full-time and want to finish a book. Unless you're writing your novel in 140 characters at a time (Don't laugh, several people wrote stories this way with other people when Twitter first came out), the time you are spending on Twitter and Facebook could be spent writing.

That's my opinion. I'm sharing what's worked for me. What might work for you could be different. Simply look at the hours in your day and see what works best.

Book Reviews

Part of a successful book launch is earning positive book reviews. Amazon helps rank books by the high number of positive reviews over the first several days (to weeks) after your book launches. I have been writing and publishing books for years, but I have found that having readers post in multiple platforms can be extremely challenging to do. Instead, I've focused on Amazon because that is where most of my readers are.

Before you begin rolling out the tactics you've planned to obtain positive book reviews, think through the strategy. If you plan on Amazon being your main source of sales, then plan for that. If you are intending to go wide with your launch, then be ready to provide direct links to how readers can leave reviews on all the different websites where your books are sold.

Before we get into the details, let's take a moment to step back and survey the land. The time to plan for reviews is way before your launch. You'll need time to write your emails, plan, and then send out follow ups.

When I launched my first book, I took an extremely long and drawn-out approach to getting book reviews. I split my approach into two options:

1.   I researched book reviewers who had blogs and wrote them directly. I kept a spreadsheet and reached out to more than 100 bloggers. I emailed ebooks or mailed physical copies of my book to as many people as I could.
2.   I added a page in the back of my ebook with a link to leaving a review.

There are a couple of problems with each of those approaches. For option one, the amount of time it took for me to do the research and then email everyone (and follow up) did not translate into a positive return on investment. Back in 2011, the switch had already begun: Bloggers were receiving more requests to review books than they had time. I did receive about a dozen bloggers who agreed to review my book, and I'm happy about that, but I spent more time on this than I would have liked.

Leaving a link in the back of the book was a simple thing to do, but it translated into so few reviews that I didn't see much success.

If I were just starting out now, I would do things a bit differently. When I look back and see that I gave away 40,000 copies of *Lost* but only have 134 reviews, I want to hang my head down in shame. Still, we live and we learn. I'm hoping you can learn from my mistake.

What I would do over is settling up a work stream that helps me and is automated. Instead of me doing all the manual work, I could have created a means for those 40,000 readers to have an easy way to leave a review.

How?

First, I would have thought through my launch approach differently. I released *Lost* after eighteen months of hard work and then spent too many months working on promotion, getting reviews, and other marketing-related tasks post book launch. What would have been more effective is the following:

- Write *Lost*
- Hold off on publishing it
- Write *Stolen* (book two)
- Publish *Lost*
- Publish *Stolen* two to three months after *Lost*
- Write *Found* (book three) in the series and publish it three to four months after *Stolen*

How would this have helped me get reviews? Simple. I could have provided an email list opt-in link in the front and back of the ebook version of *Lost* (book one).

I could then also have provided an incentive to either give book one away through Facebook ads, Instafree (To be fair to myself, this site didn't exist back in 2011, but it does now.) and work on indie author email list shares.

Instead of giving the book away on Amazon (where I didn't have a way of collecting those 40,000 readers' email addresses), I could have built a marketing funnel to offer interested readers an incentive.

Let's walk this through step by step.

With book one and two out in your series, you could offer book one for free for a limited time. Simply build a landing page on your website with an offer to give the book away for free once the person signs up to your email list.

Connect your webpage via a link or (as I can with Squarespace.com) connect a form on your website to your email list provider. Since I use Mailchimp, I created the following page:

Ronvitale.com/lost-1

A potential reader lands there, clicks on the nice and green "Send My Free Book!" button, and lands on another page that asks them for their email address. The interested reader puts in their email address, confirms they opted in via email and they're now on your subscriber list, and they get book one for free.

We're almost finished!

Next create your email automation workflow. I use the following:

- Welcome and free story or book
- Share a story that aligns to your brand. My books tell stories about strong female heroines who don't need a man to save them.
-
- I sent them a fun poll that's tied to my brand.
- I ask them to buy a book.
- My next email gives them an option of unsubscribing and lets them know what type of content I'm going to keep sending them.
- I ask for a book review.

Now let's put this all together:

I can set up a campaign on Instafreebie (a service that allows you to give your book away for free but collects a reader's email address, sending that information to your email list provider). The power involved in that is amazing.

Once I have a campaign set up on Instafreebie, I can then network with indie authors in the same genre and we can help each other out by sending our promotions to our subscriber lists. If I work with five authors, my promotion will be sent to five subscriber lists, one from each author, and I'll send the five book offers to my list. It's a win-win for everyone.

A reader gets a book for free, you get a subscriber, and all the other authors increase their subscribers too.

The beauty of the plan is that the email automation is set up once and is working for you while you're at your full-time job, out with the family having a good time, or when you're sleeping. It just works. Email automation is an amazing thing.

The power behind a service like Mailchimp or Aweber (or similar email subscriber platforms) is that you can create automated emails as simple or as complex as you would like. Since I just started using automation in 2016, reader engagement (open rates and clicks) has increased. I've started off small and have a lot yet to learn, but there's great flexibility and opportunity ahead.

If you are new and are screaming out to the wild that you don't have an email list yet and can't get other authors to work with you, fear not. I've seen subscribers come to my list simply by having a free offer made available on Instafreebie.

Another option is to run Facebook ads and drive the traffic directly to your sign-up landing page. A reader sees your Facebook ad, clicks on it, lands on your website, signs up to your subscriber list, and then, over time, receives your automated emails.

What's happening here is that you've created a marketing funnel for yourself and over time, you can market your products to your list. When a subscriber gets book one for free and then sees "ads" inside listing that book two is now for sale, that reader has more of an incentive to buy your next book if they like your writing. And with your automated emails offering readers other free offers, you can slowly build your relationship with people.

Instead of simply going up to strangers and saying: "Buy all my books," you're taking the time to get to know readers over time by sending them emails over weeks and months that are valuable and authentic. The best way to learn how to do this is to subscribe to another indie author's list and learn what they're doing.

Advance Reader Copy (ARC)

When you publish your first book, finding people to accept an ARC from you and then write a review might be challenging. For *Lost*, I didn't have many options. I had no one on my subscriber list.

However, that's slowly changed over time. If you're starting out, it's never too early to build your list.

Personally, I like to handle all my own ebook formatting because I like the control it gives me. When I am publishing a book, I create an ARC copy and then a "to be sold" ebook version of my book. In the ARC, I list a thank you at the end and instructions about how the person could leave a review.

Think of it this way: When you're working on publishing a book, that book becomes your world. You're tied into deadlines, are stressed with 101 things, but for ARC readers, that's not a top priority in their life. I've had people say they want to read my book and then decide they don't have time. Or, they'll read the book and not have time to leave a review. With my subscriber list, I often take a segment of my more engaged readers and then offer them the option of receiving an ARC.

I then make a list as a Google sheet of those individuals who agreed to read the book and leave a review. I clearly communicate to readers the date I'm looking for them to leave a review and send them instructions. I want to be clear: I am asking for an honest review and not begging them to leave a five-star review.

What's important to know is that Amazon has been pulling reviews that it thinks are paid ones so I ask readers to put in the following language in their review:

"I received an ARC at no cost from the author."

In networking with fellow authors, readers have reported that their reviews were deleted if other wording such as "exchange" is used.

After my email is sent out, ARCs are sent, and then I send a follow-up email. Once the review is written, I send a personalized thank you note to the reader.

Is that a lot of work? Yes, it is. If I had a virtual assistant, that person could handle this type of work, but at the moment, I do not have an assistant. Still, the building of reviews is important to ensure that your books are rising in the ranks and can attract the right readers.

A sustained increase in reviews over the days and weeks after launch has proven to help with a book's ranking. But don't take my word for it; do your own research. There are a lot of podcasts and articles out there that get into the nitty-gritty of Amazon ranking.

If you've read to this point and you're a new indie author about to launch your first book but have no subscribers on an email list and do not have a strategy in place to market your book and obtain reviews, I would ask that you reflect on your goals.

Once you launch your book, yes, it's a good feeling to know that all that hard work you put into the effort is over, but how is the book going to sell if no one knows about the book?

Build that subscriber base; it'll help you in the long run.

Advertisements

You can purchase Facebook ads, Google AdWords, Amazon ads, a Bookbub promotion, or eReader News Today (ENT) ads. There is a whole host of similar places that offer advertising options. The array of choices can be overwhelming. I've heard some authors swear by Bookbub and others say that it didn't really help them that much.

One of the most important bits of research you can perform is to understand your genre and how well it's selling. A good way to do that is to look at a Bookbub and see what they charge for a promotion and what they anticipate the return on investment will be for you. Bookbub has collected data for several years, and they'll list the price of the ad and how many people they expect will download/engage in downloading a free book or purchase your book on sale. When you see the genre you write and compare with other genres, you'll have a better sense of what's selling and what's not.

Right now, romances and thrillers are extremely popular. Fantasy books (one of the genres I write), are not as popular.

If you're working full-time like me and are about to launch your first book, I would suggest you spend little to no money on advertising. Running ads on one book might seem like a great strategy, but what else will that reader be able to buy from you? What is your overall plan once the reader buys your only book? And if you give the book away for free for several days, then what?

What would be more beneficial for you is to advertise once you have other books in your series.

Starting out can be difficult, and I'm not saying that it's a total waste of time to advertise if you only have one book, but with limited time (and I expect a limited budget), why not use your energy to get started on your next book? The best marketing you can do when you're starting out is to write more books.

Chapter 11: Reassess Your Goals

Congratulations! You launched a book. After all the hard work, there's that moment in time when you click that button to launch your baby to the world and then… Many authors, myself included, experience doubt and fear. Did you do the right thing? What if someone you know reads the book and thinks you crazy? What if the book doesn't sell? What if, what if, what if?

It's normal to go through a period of intense speculation, but the challenge is: What are you going to do about it?

Some authors brush the doubt aside, jump back in the saddle, and start the next book immediately.

I'm not like that. I propose taking two to three days off to smell the roses and relax. After my book launches, I need to get caught up with the rest of my life. Because I work full-time at a day job, I still have deadlines and the tasks associated with them, and I also have the chores around the house. If it's spring/summer when I finish a book, I like to work in the garden or mow the lawn. In the fall/winter, I rake leaves or find some sort of activity to do around the house (painting, cleaning—something that takes my mind off my book's launch).

I like to disconnect from writing and give myself an opportunity to decompress.

Remember the early parts of this book in which I talk about the connections you have with your mind, body, and soul? When I launch a book, I like to take stock and reflect. How off the rails was I in meeting my book launch deadline? Did I start to fray at the end, snapping at my family because of the pressure, or did all go well? How do I feel? Happy, sad, overwhelmed—a mixture of that and so much more?

I like to reflect and then reassess my writing goals. After a book launch, I find it a good time to see whether I need to change course or stay firm on my path.

Dig Out the Business Plan

Crack open the plan and read it through. Are the goals you've wanted to achieve still obtainable? Have you moved closer to your goal?

For me, I'm writing for the long haul. I'm still in the early phases of my writing career. I've put in seven years of hard work, but I want to pace myself, ensuring that I do not burn out or have a meltdown. I want to look at my business plan and be honest with myself:

Am I happy?

Before you write another word, plan your next book, or spend another dollar on a marketing promotion, how did you answer that question? Are you truly happy? Or are you overwhelmed, stressed, and unsure how to move forward?

Let's be honest: Many authors will launch a book and have such high hopes that their book will sell like gangbusters and then reality hits—a few sales and then flat line. I've had it happen to me, and it's not a good feeling. When my sales have trickled to almost nil and then flat lined, I've panicked. I've looked around and found what other authors are doing to get sales, and I've thrown myself at that. Wasting time, money, and just chasing after more sales. But is that truly making me happy?

Sure, some of you who are reading this book will make a lot of money selling books, but not all of you will. For the majority of writers, earning an income will be extremely challenging. It's not impossible, but it will take time. There have been days when I've said to my wife: "If I would have taken a job at McDonald's, I would have made more money than I've made so far from selling books." But is that the right question to ask?

What are your goals and how are you going to get there? Once I've launched a book, if I don't stop to think and reflect, then I'm putting myself in danger of burning out. The real secret is that you can't work a full-time job, write full-time, spend time with your family, have a healthy social life, research marketing, write emails for your subscribers, engage with your readers, and still sleep at night. There are steps you can take to automate some of the work that you'll need to do, but I believe there needs to be a healthy balance.

So many writers try to power on through the rough times, but what is there to power through? Years of hard work? Spending all your time and energy on writing? Is it really worth it? If you're a parent, are you making time to spend with your kids? Or are you so focused on your writing and full-time job that you've sacrificed all else in your life?

It doesn't matter if you are single, your kids are off at college, you don't have kids, or whatever your circumstance, the point is that having a healthy balance in life will make you a better writer. Experience the world, talk with people, engage, live, go to the movies, read a book, learn to juggle—whatever it is that you like in the world, do not give that up. Fight for that time with every ounce of strength in your body! Fight!

To give our soul only to work and not to fully engage in life can be crippling to look back on. You can't earn back the time that you've lost. But you can make changes today.

Commit to Yourself

I firmly believe in making a commitment to yourself to live a healthy and whole life. We have such a short amount of time on this Earth, and as much as I love writing, I need to make time to do other things. Cranking five books out in a year might be possible for you, but is it healthy? Only you can answer that question.

Working full-time at a day job and then carving out time to write (and market a book and everything else that comes with being an indie author) is not easy to do. We're not talking about working hard for eighteen months; we're talking about decades. Let that sink in for a moment. Are you in this for the long haul or not?

This is why I believe it's important to reassess your writing goals after you launch a book. Listen to yourself. Take a walk and let your mind wander. If your body is telling you that you need to take a break, then do it. A marathon is not simply run all in one day. The training for the race takes place months before. Being an author takes practice at your craft and has probably already included years of schooling and reading. Now you're at a point to look yourself in the mirror and decide: Is this where I want to be? Is it really?

I cannot identify with writers who are just churning books out solely to make a profit. That's not what motivates me to get up at 5:00 a.m. to write or squeeze time out over lunch. I write because I want to make a difference in the world. I want to share stories that will not only entertain people but inspire.

If you're working at a day job full-time but still want to be a writer, I expect that there are many reasons for why you want to write.

Are you being true to yourself and what you want out of life? Or are you disappointed, exhausted, and feel lost? Take stock, truly think about what you want, and then commit to yourself.

When I sit down to write, I often feel a surge of joy run through me, but there are also mornings when I struggle to get the words out. I still show up and make my writing goal. I push and sometimes I need to push hard. I do not want to continue struggling if I'm not happy. There is no harm in saying you need to take a break or no longer want to be a writer. It's your life and you can do what you want.

These are hard questions to answer and might seem strange coming from me in a book teaching you how to be successful. But would you rather be happy in your life or depressed and overwhelmed?

Be honest with yourself and commit to what you want in life.

Hone Your Craft

One of the most difficult things for me to do is to go back and read one of my early novels. I look at how far I've come with my writing and want to cringe at some parts of the first stories I wrote. In fact, on a recent monthly conference call with fellow indie authors, I joked with other callers about how that is one of the most torturous actions for me: Put me in a room and force me to read my own early works. I just shiver to think about it.

Why?

I am not a perfect writer and am working hard on bettering my plotting, dialogue, and character development. Writing, and becoming good at it—really good at it—takes many years and lots of practice. The average catch phrase that I've heard many writers share among themselves is that your first 1,000,000 words are crap, and then you'll start to hit your stride. Now, I don't know if I'd go that far, but I like the sentiment.

When I sat down and wrote *Lost*, I didn't really know what I needed to do. Yes, I had written *Dorothea's Song*, but the first draft of that was written back in 1987. I started *Lost* in 2009, so a lot of time had passed. The style of *Lost* is dramatically different than any of my other books. I chose to explore the epistolary style of writing. I completed the book and then decided that I wouldn't be doing that again.

By the time I wrote *Stolen*, I had learned a thing or two about pacing and character development, but I still have so much to learn. All of this hit home to me when I asked my wife to read *Lost*. She finished it and said, "Well, I can tell that you were tired a lot when you wrote the book." I didn't know what she meant, and she pointed out to me that Cinderella often says, "I'm tired" or "I'm exhausted" throughout *Lost*. I hadn't seen the duplication or the thread that I had woven through the book, and once it was pointed out to me, I read through the book and better understood what I had done.

There are grammar rules: active/passive verbs, dialogue tags, transitions, show and don't tell, and the list goes on and on. I work hard trying to understand the rules of grammar, but it's also important to know when to break them (especially in dialogue to better capture actual speech). One of the biggest challenges for me in writing Cinderella and capturing her voice was to write as a woman and to find a balance on more formalized speech since my Cinderella novels take place in the late eighteenth and early nineteenth centuries.

Over the years I have done the following: Obtained a B.A. in English literature and French, earned my M.A. in English literature, taken creative writing classes, signed up for writing workshops, read "how to" writing books, and participated in a writing group to have my work critiqued, but one of the most important lessons I've learned that truly helps me is a simple thing to do and I love it—read.

Stephen King has said: "If you don't have time to read, you don't have the time (or the tools) to write."

Now I'm not a fan of Stephen King. I spent years getting through the *Dark Tower* series, and when I finished the last book and went beyond the part where King says that the story is over, I turned the page, and when I did, well, let's just say I wanted to throw the book against the wall. If I ever meet you in person, we can have a drink and sit down and discuss that ending. But I digress.

I may not run out and buy Stephen King books, but I did read his *On Writing: A Memoir of the Craft* and found it an extremely helpful book for me to understand what it's like to actually be an author and the work that's needed.

I've read enough of King's books (all of the *Dark Tower* series) to study his style and better understand why he's so successful. I've seen the themes and patterns that he builds up in his books and can better see the emotional threads he knits into the stories he tells. He's a master storyteller and there's a lot to learn from him.

But there's also much for me to learn by reading other writers. My thesis work *Memory and the Quest for Self* is a study of selected works of Margaret Atwood and Alice Walker. The seeds of all my novels can be found in that thesis work. I wanted to write about how people who have gone through trauma find a way toward healing by telling their stories to others. They own the abuse and suffering that was inflicted on them and overcome their pasts by shedding the shackles to grow into strong, healthy women.

Over the years, I've read *Beowulf,* Homer's *The Odyssey,* French literature, *Les Fleurs du Mal* by Baudelaire, non-fiction, fiction, science fiction, mysteries, fantasy, and everything in between. More recently, I've made a conscious effort to diversify my reading by buying books outside of my normal area of interest. I study the Hugo and Nebula award winners and pick them up each year so that I can better understand what is winning awards and why. (I've thoroughly enjoyed Nnedi Okorafor's *Binti.* Her book expertly captures a unique voice and perspective. Well worth a read!)

All of this reading takes time. Here is where reality kicks in. There are only twenty-four hours in the day. When I finish a book and reassess my goals, I also like to look at my life in general. How much am I reading? The honest answer is that I'm not reading enough. I use the time on my commute to and from my full-time day job to read, but many times I'm also trying to read non-fiction. I'm trying to learn more about publishing, copyright, indie publishing, writing, marketing, and self-help-style books (of the likes of Brené Brown and Elizabeth Gilbert).

When I notice that I've not carved time out to read fiction, I take stock of what I'd like to read and then make more time to do that. But it's not easy. I also enjoy films and TV. I've read, to date, all the George R. R. Martin *Fire and Ice* books and have watched every episode of *Game of Thrones.* I enjoyed comparing the books with the HBO series because I can see where the editors (thankfully!) revised the storyline to trim it down.

One of my earliest memories as a kid is entwined with reading. My stepfather's brother gave me some of Isaac Asimov's science fiction books, and my world exploded into a whole different creative path. Sure, I read Tolkien and fell in love with Middle Earth, but I had never truly explored the world of science fiction. Yes, I love *Star Wars,* but that's more fantasy than hard science fiction to me. Asimov's books opened new possibilities for me, and I discovered he had written hundreds of books, on everything from the Bible to Shakespeare to all sorts of other genres. Over time I realized I did not have to limit myself to writing only one genre. I could write both fantasy and science fiction. I could just write. And now I do.

For me, I like to understand what patterns and themes are in the various genre books, learn from that, and then decide if I want to break those rules or follow them. Each book I read is a journey for me to another time and place where I can experience something that I might never see or feel in my life, but through imagination, I can partake in the most intimate parts of a character's life. I can't learn any of this if I don't read.

Invest in You

The book is written and launched, the road stretches before you, and now what? What do you want to do next? Does it make sense to write the next book? Do you have a series planned, a new series you'd like to start, or want to write non-fiction? The twenty-first century is filled with opportunities for authors, but before I make any decisions, I like to have a better grasp of my long-term plan. I like to make time to process my experience, reflect, and see what I could do differently.

I have written book after book over the last eight years, and now I've discovered that I need to learn more about how to build my readership. I can write in obscurity, but I want more than that. I have goals of being a best-selling author and want to engage with my readers. I've a small following now, and I want to grow that.

Before I started this book, I made a conscious choice. I had just launched *Faith: The Jovian Gate Chronicles* to the world and could have started book two of the series or jumped back to write the next *Cinderella's Secret Witch Diaries* book. I have a whole list of ideas and plans that I wrote down last year in my business plan, but I threw all that away to write this book. Why?

I wanted to take stock of what I had learned and then share that with fellow authors. I have learned a lot, things I didn't even know I could learn, about marketing, formatting ebooks, and setting up my email list. I have taken time over the last eight years to learn. Learn by doing. I have sought out people to help me, asked questions, read blogs, thanked people for help, and decided I wanted to give back to people just like me.

But at the core of it all, this book is my way of ruminating about my journey so far. I have wanted to write down what I've learned, take stock, hold it in my hands, and see what has worked and what hasn't. The biggest challenge for me is discoverability. How do I let readers know about my books and then have them buy my novels? How?

The only way I know how to do that is to invest time, lots of time, into learning new skills:

Learning email marketing, creating a sales funnel, engaging with your readers on forums/Facebook groups, and building your brand.

Seems overwhelming, right? Yes, it does. I freely admit that sometimes my head is ready to explode with everything that I need to learn. But what is need? What is a "should" or a "must"?

Remember, back in the early portion of the book, the sections about the mind, body and soul? Now is when you'll need what you learned in that section the most. Writing a book and publishing it, yes, it's hard, but the adrenaline kicks in, and you can plow on through to get the work done. After the book has launched, then what? Where do you really want to go from here?

Investing in yourself allows you the opportunity to open new doors that you do not even know are possible. The good news is that you now have the skills you need to succeed. But the difficult part is practicing these skills, continuing to make them part of your daily ritual, and remaining grounded.

I wrote and launched three books and fell into a steady pattern. But when I started writing *The Witch's Coven* series, I had not learned yet to apply healthy habits on having a good work-life balance. I simply looked at my life and turned everything up to eleven. I burned the candle at both ends because I believed I was going to "push through." If I only worked harder, then I would "make it" and be the best-selling author that I wanted.

But working harder isn't the same thing as working smarter.

All the successful indie authors I network with have made it to where they are today because they not only are writers but they understand the business of writing. If you have no one to sell your books to (or have anyone to promote your books for you), then how are you going to sell them?

Invest in yourself. Watch webinars to teach you what a sales funnel is and how to create a strategy for a successful email marketing campaign, and step out of being an author to remember what you would like as a reader. How would you like the authors you like to engage and contact you? Do you simply want to be sold to? Or do you want something more?

Though it's not the purview of this book to go into the nitty-gritty of these topics, let me at least cover them and give an overview to help you.

Who Are You?

The word brand is tossed around a lot, and I think it's worth taking some time to explore. The easiest method to define your brand is to simply have you ask yourself: Why do you write? What do you stand for? For example, if you write extremely violent books about zombies for a more mature audience, you probably would not want to act in a way that goes against what you believe. If one day you release a book about brain-eating zombies and the next you are focusing on children's stories, sharing pictures of flowers and platitudes to those on your email list, well, this might confuse your readership.

Another way to look at this: If you just released a brain-eating zombie book and then share a review about the latest zombie movie, that's more aligned to not only the topic that you write but how you deliver the content to your readers, which is also important. Your author persona is the whole package.

For me, I write books about strong female characters who overcome challenges and realize they do not need a man to save them. I also share stories about my life to support that theme. I want the world to see what I stand for and why and stay consistent with that message over time.

Think of the big companies in the world: Nike, Apple, McDonald's, etc. Each of those companies has a brand associated with their image. Nike promotes itself as being active, fit, and willing to take on challenges. If you were to see a Nike commercial with people sitting on a sofa reading, you might be confused. The brand that Nike has spent hundreds of millions of dollars on over the decades is clear and true for them.

When creating your brand—who you want to be to the world, how you engage with readers, and your overall public persona—remember to be authentic and true to yourself.

Email Marketing

Choose an email marketing platform, sign up, and start experimenting. An extremely simple way to get started is to put a sign-up page on your website and have links in the back of your books. What you are looking to do is to create a sales funnel to get leads. You want to engage with people, invite them to join your mailing list, and then share with those readers on a regular schedule. You're looking to build a relationship with your readers. And in order to do that, you'll need a content strategy. What I do is mix up my emails between a promotion for me and sharing free promotions from other indie authors as well as sharing topics that support my brand. I've written about dealing with anxiety, stress, handling problems, and overcoming obstacles. The topics I choose to write about match closely with the themes in my books. Think about what you want to write about and how that can support you.

Now that you have an idea of what you want to share, take time to write up a simple editorial calendar. Start off with a plan. Will you send emails out to your subscribers once a month or every week? Pick a plan and stick with it. Add that work into your production schedule over the course of the year.

The granular "to-do" list on creating an email list can take up a lot of time. To save you from some of the mistakes that I made, I can tell you that if I could do it all over again, I would have built an automation chain. When I first started to build my list, I opted for the free Mailchimp plan that didn't allow me to use automation tools. Sure, I could manually create an email and then schedule it to go out whenever I wanted, but using the automation features in an email platform brings you peace of mind.

Now, when a subscriber signs up, they receive a series of emails over a period of time. Earlier in the book, I explained the details of my emails.

Your Funnel

Eventually you want to sell products to your readers. Those products might be print books, ebooks, audiobooks, T-shirts, or whatever. Unless you have a list of people to build a relationship with and then eventually sell to, you will continually be dependent on outside sources for sales. Yes, getting a Bookbub is great, but it's only one arrow in your quiver. Same with Facebook and a whole other host of tools. A good strategy is to integrate your marketing to funnel people to your opt-in email list page. Once readers are part of your list, then they're in your "funnel," and you can send them emails, use the intelligence you see from their engagement to create segments, and then send certain people more emails or special offers, depending on what emails they open.

That's the power of having a marketing strategy and building your sales funnel. If done right, you can set it up and have a passive way of making sales when you're sleeping because emails can be sent out as part of your automation plan. Yes, setting all this up takes time, and I got a few gray hairs over it, but I've learned a lot over the last year, and it's made all the difference.

Chapter 12: Dealing with Change

Publishing has changed dramatically in the last ten years. I expect that the industry will continue to change for the next ten. Technological advances, changing reader habits, and the globalization and democratization of the production of content continue to disrupt.

I look back and remember being seventeen years old and asking my grandfather to lend me $10,000. I had received a contract from a vanity press to publish my first novel *Dorothea's Song*. If I paid the press, the low, low price of $10,000, I would see my book in print. Vanity presses back in the '80s were a joke because essentially they were ego trips for authors. Once your paid the fee, you'd get your book (boxes and boxes of them), and they would sit in your garage because no one would actually buy them since you wouldn't have a distribution platform.

My grandfather was right to deny me the money and think me crazy. At the time, I remember feeling hurt, frustrated, and just wanting a way to have my book see the light of day. I can still recall how emotional I felt in reading the contract that the vanity press had sent me and seeing my book's title and my name listed there. I wanted my book to see the light of day so badly, but I didn't know how. Now through indie publishing, anyone can publish a book, in hours, for hardly any money. If you have an account with one of the major platforms (Nook Press, Kobo, iBookstore, or Amazon), you can upload your file and sell it to the world. The opportunity is there, with millions of people doing it, but most authors do not have wild success.

The hardest part isn't necessarily writing the book or formatting it but the marketing. Change is always in front of us. People are using their mobile devices more and more. Reading time is competing with watching Netflix on the train or playing the latest app. Competition is fierce and what worked today may not work tomorrow.

Stay the Course

After you have reassessed your goals and taken stock of whether or not to adjust your production schedule for your next book, you'll probably want to write another. When I finished *Lost*, I needed some time to figure out what I wanted to do, plan the plot (at least in my head) for *Stolen*, and then write. But I made some decisions along the way that helped me stay strong and remain true to my goal of being an author. I didn't give up when my book didn't make the best-seller's list. I needed a plan but had no idea of what to do, where to go, and how best to move forward.

All I knew is that I didn't want to give up and wanted to keep trying. So I did.

I set my goal to be an indie author and became one. I decided to follow the path in front of me by writing and adapting along the way. I did not simply put blinders on, write my books, publish them, and then refuse to change, grow, or adapt. I thought of myself as a tree that could bend in the wind. I needed to be flexible and visualized myself on a journey that I could not see the end.

The hardest part for me is the realization that there wasn't an easy fix or quick road to success. The news media focused on the stories of the few indie authors who made six-figure salaries, but the rest of us, well, we were left to find our own way. The question that you'll need to ask yourself at some point is:

Should I give up? Is it healthy for me to continue?

The answer to this question is more complicated than I had ever imagined. I have stopped writing for years at a time, but I haven't stopped since 2008. I started writing *Lost* and took some time off to do marketing and then started up with *Stolen*.

You might decide that writing isn't for you. You tried it, gave it your best, but want to stop. Choosing to no longer be an author is fine. There is no shame in giving up—if that's what you really want to do.

There is a difference between being healthy and unhealthy. Ask yourself whether you are growing and changing or locked and rigid within your creativity. Be honest with yourself.

The famous quote to describe insanity is: "doing the same thing over and over again and expecting different results."

I've thought about that as I continue to publish my books. I work hard, write, and release a book, but I continue to grow by learning new skills, tactics, and ways of applying them to my marketing plan.

I am simply not cranking out a book and expecting the world to discover it. I am working hard on a strategy to connect me with my readers.

If you have reached a point in which the writing isn't fun any longer, then maybe staying the course isn't healthy for you. Take a break, reassess, meditate, and think through what you want out of life. If you do have a full-time job, what is that job and why do you keep doing it? Is it because you need the money and you're stuck there or are you really bringing value to the job and love what you do?

With writing: No one forced me to get up at 5:35 a.m. this morning to come down and write. I chose that. I wanted to write. There's a need for me to write because I believe I can share what I've learned and hope some of what I now know can help others. I choose to stay the course because I love what I do. If you don't, then stop. There are authors who have written a book and then chose to go into editing, story development, marketing, or book formatting. There are many paths to remain creative and stay in indie publishing. What your path will become might surprise you. Allow yourself the room to discover what works best for you.

The Power of Us

In 2015, I learned that "It's not possible to do it all." No matter how hard I tried, I could not do everything that I needed or "should" do in the course of a regular day. I would either need to sacrifice sleep, clone myself, or travel through time to meet all of my goals. One of those options would be detrimental to my health, and the other two haven't been invented yet.

What I learned in 2016 is an amendment to 2015's lesson. My mantra for 2016 was:

"With help from others, I can do it all."

I made some big leaps forward in 2016, and it's by coming out of my shell and taking a risk. I chose to leave my solitary world of writing and branch out by networking with other indie authors. I didn't simply work on my own, reading books and watching webinars, but I tweeted directly to authors, shared tips with them, congratulated them on their successes, or shared their tweets and promotions.

I chose to engage and put myself out into the world by offering help, listening, and being a resource when needed. Kristine Kathryn Rusch linked to my 2015 year-end wrap-up blog post on her website, and in 2016 Joanna Penn invited me on her podcast. How did this happen? I didn't simply blindly email them. I worked over time by reading what they wrote, listening to Penn's podcast and then provided value by offering useful information to them. I did my homework and shared it.

In other areas, I stumbled upon a private Facebook group of fellow authors and started participating in a monthly conference call. I shared what I knew about Google Analytics and learned a lot about setting up newsletters and book launches. By being in that one Facebook group, I began searching for other groups until I had connected with more indie authors.

Over time, I could then ask for help because I had provided assistance to others. Instead of going to fellow authors with my hat in hand begging for help, I could reach out to someone with an offer of mutual assistance or provide value with the knowledge I had gained. Instead of waiting for the world to discover me, I learned in 2016 that I could be active and work with fellow authors. But after nine months of hard work in networking, helping others, and being present and seen in the community, I reached out and asked others if they would participate in an email swap with me.

And several authors said yes, and that's made all the difference to me.

An email swap is the most simplistic thing and extremely helpful. I approached an author who had published books similar to my own and asked if she would be willing to send a promotion about my free book to her email list. Her readers would have the opportunity to download my free book once they subscribed to my mailing list, and in return, I would promote a book by the author. Everyone wins.

No actual email addresses are shared; each author simply sends an email out to their subscribers talking up the promotion.

Early in 2016, I tried sharing blog posts, inviting several authors to be a guest on my blog. In return, I wrote articles for them. I tried that for several months but saw no traction in blog traffic or email subscribers. I changed my tactic and reached out to ask for the email share. The first time I tried a promotion, the author I worked with had a big success and I had only several dozen new subscribers.

I tried again and a best-selling author agreed to work with me. On Labor Day weekend, my family and I were away on vacation when I rolled out of bed, checked my email, and saw that I had more than 300 emails that had poured in over several minutes. Each email represented a new subscriber. A bell went off in my head, and I learned two things:

1. People who offer to help rock!
2. Work can take place while I slept.

Over the course of one day, I gained nearly 1,000 new subscribers. That's nearly 1,000 new readers who I had a chance to build a relationship with and engage, and these readers had now begun to receive my automated emails. I could have continued along my path and written my books and refused to grow and change, but then I would have missed out on an opportunity to broaden my reach, learn successful marketing tactics, and help others.

What I love so much about the indie author community is the willingness for members to help each other. Resources can be pooled and information shared, and we can all learn together what works and what doesn't. I am now in a Facebook group of indie authors where people are sharing screenshots of their sales dashboard, talking through what they did to succeed.

Help is out there, willing and able, but how I chose to approach the community has made all the difference to me. I am looking to learn but also give back. I wanted to make certain I brought my own wealth of knowledge to the table when talking with other authors. I approached my networking from an area of strength and some confidence rather than in weakness.

When I started out back in 2008, I didn't feel like I had a lot to offer, but over the years, I have learned a lot from my day job and from all the training I've done on the side. I now have skills I can share with others and help them. I firmly believe in the "pay it forward" mentality. When I tried podcasting, I had a fellow podcaster help me learn how to use the recording software. I remember how he sent me his own private "how to" document, and I used that to create a podcast that I ran for more than five years.

Years later I offer assistance by answering questions from fellow authors about indie publishing, analytics, and social media. I would not be where I am today without the help I received from others, and I want to give back.

In looking back, 2016 was a pivotal year for my writing career because I now see possibilities where I had once only seen closed doors. Instead of being negative in accepting that I can't do it all, now I see that by learning new skills, I don't have to be awake twenty-four-seven always working, but I can set up automation emails and work with fellow indie authors to network and help each other out. Possibilities are created because I now see that I have opportunities by talking and listening to others. I'm learning more than I ever expected possible.

My plan is to continue reaching out and network even more. To do that, I want to attend conferences so that I can meet face to face with other authors, listen to their talks, and then form partnerships and create new opportunities for both of us.

Networking

But how can you do this if you don't know any authors, haven't published a book yet, and have zero subscribers on your mailing list? I remember thinking the same thing years ago. The whole process of indie publishing was a mystery to me. Back then, the news media focused on the big success stories. What I would hear was how authors like Amanda Hocking scored a seven-figure deal with a publishing house and how she "came out of nowhere."

I decided to do some homework and researched Hocking's background. On her blog, she wrote about the hard work she put into networking with people on blogs and in forums and how she had not just written her books, but she had found a way to match those books with the right readers. That gave me hope because the true story wasn't that she wrote a few books and her success came soon after. No, she put a lot of hard work into building her audience.

For me, I made several missteps in the early part of my career. I gave more than 40,000 ebook copies away of *Lost* and did not receive people's email addresses before they received the book. Now I use Instafreebie and a form on my website to collect subscribers to my mailing list. Those two forms are tied into my Mailchimp account.

If you are starting at zero, the only way to go is up. The hard work that needs to take place before you start selling books is to sit down and write. Unless you have written a novel before, the first time is going to be hard. There are a hundred different things to learn, and that fuzzy middle of the book might be more of a challenge than you expect.

Give yourself time to learn the process, but do your homework along the way. Listen to indie publishing podcasts. I list a whole set of resources in the early part of the book. Subscribe to the podcasts and the mailing lists of people like Joanna Penn and Kristine Kathryn

Rusch but also subscribe to the lists of fellow authors you like. Study what the successful writers are doing. Follow them on Twitter and Facebook and read their email newsletters. Buy the ebooks that are selling well in your genre and study them. Look at the front and back parts of the book, see what offers are being advertised in those books, and pay attention to the covers.

While you're doing all that work, join some Facebook, Goodreads, and KBoards.com groups with like-minded authors in them as well as groups for readers interested in the topics that interest you. If you write epic fantasy, join groups with similar readers. What you'll want to do is to join in the conversation, engage with people, and eventually, in subtle ways, share that you're a writer without sounding like a used car salesman. I would recommend that you list your website in your signature for a forum and eventually the books that you have written (KBoards.com allows you to put the images of your books in your signature as well as links to them).

Then be yourself. Talk with people, comment on things, and join in the conversation. The purpose of all this work is to connect you with where your tribe hangs out. What doesn't work, and trust me, because I was called out on this, is writing a blog post that subtly works in your book you're trying to sell and putting that blog post in the forum. Admins smell that type of hard sell from a mile away.

Be authentic and engage, and over time, you'll make connections. I have worked hard to bring value to people by answering questions, commenting intelligently, and sharing others' blog posts. There are more authors to follow than I have time to list. Study the Amazon best-selling list, pick an author, and see if she has a blog. If she does, follow what she writes about and follow her on Twitter.

The approach in networking might seem difficult and time consuming because it is. But gradually making connections with people is a much more natural approach than to find five authors and then hound them with newbie questions. Again, take a step back and think about the approach. Imagine if you were a best-selling author and you had dozens of new authors tweeting and emailing you for help. I doubt you'd want to help a stranger. Sending cold emails out to best-selling authors asking them to share your new book to their subscribers isn't a great approach.

Maybe to flip things: Start a blog and ask to interview the author. I've reached out to authors, and when I do, I send them five questions via email, ask them for a photo and what book they'd like to push, and offer a generous deadline. The approach works because you'd be bringing value to the author. In the meantime, the questions that you ask can help you. Post the interview up on your blog, and try another author for next month. Over time, you'll build a nice collection of interviews for your blog which can help you answer the questions you have.

Networking doesn't have to be scary, but it does mean that you take a risk. You'll need to send an email out to an author at some point, send a tweet, or respond to a forum post. Balancing a day job, family responsibility, writing, and learning the business side of publishing all at the same time isn't easy. I've found the work to be fun but time management to be extremely difficult. If you're not working on your book and are spending too much time networking, you'll not have a book to sell.

Go back to your business plan, think about your long-term strategy, and stick to those goals. Sure, adjust as necessary, but stay focused. Just because a certain genre is selling well today doesn't mean you should drop everything and try to do the same thing.

Surrounding myself with a community has helped me realize there are people who are willing to help and offer advice, but most importantly, there are many authors willing to share how their book launches went, what worked, and what didn't. You simply need to join a Facebook group or two and follow along in the conversation. Start small, provide value, and keep trying.

Chapter 13: Starting Over Again

Maybe you finished your first book and want to start the next or maybe you wrote 500 words and need to repeat the process again and again and again. Either way, you'll need to figure out a process of how to continue the work each and every day.

I've been studying writing for decades now, and that still doesn't make me a fantastic writer. I realize I have a lifelong journey ahead of me and choose to see the world as one of several possibilities. There's always something new for me to learn, share, and be. I like that. Definitely makes life interesting.

Through my schooling at university and the writing and marketing books/blogs I've read, I noticed a pattern to the work. Many books come with exercises, worksheets, and the like. I have dutifully completed those exercises in order to strengthen my skills, but let's be honest: How many people get to the end of the book and actually do those exercises? Be honest with yourself.

If you're one of the people who does the work, then you have solid self-discipline, and that teaching style works for you. But I bet there are many more of you who throw up your hands in frustration and just want to see a plan. Maybe you think: Show me what to do and I'll do it; or Light the path for me and I'll follow it. Unfortunately, running a business isn't like that.

There will be days when you get up in the morning, and you'll want to skip writing. The heavy workload of the day job will pull on you as will the commitments to family and running a household. The weight will be heavy and you might skip a day, then two, give yourself off a week, then a month, and time flies by without any progress being made.

The concept of being a best-selling writer is a beautiful dream to hold in your mind. You can get by through the hard days at the full-time job by telling yourself, "One day I'll write my book..." I'm here to tell you the truth. The books you want to write will never get written unless you sit your butt down and get to work. And, guess what? The truth is that the work is going to be hard.

I lost years of time in my twenties and thirties writing only when I felt like it. I would write a story because my muse spoke to me, and then I'd try to get the short story published. My reasoning went like this: If I write some short stories and get them published, then I can use that momentum to help me get noticed by publishing companies. Then I can write another book. I fooled myself into thinking that my power and strength could be given to me by a nameless entity. Through the magic of traditional publishing, the writing gods would bestow favor upon me, and I would succeed. I didn't know how that would happen, but surely, after all the schooling I went through, someone would discover me.

Over the years, I have needed to start over. Not just once, but several times. I realized that I needed to make a committed effort to write and that the best way to do that wasn't simply wishing I could be a writer but to be one. I started to write on a more regular basis, I surrounded myself with positive influences (listened to writing podcasts, watched "how to" marketing webinars, and read lots of books) and chose to break through my view of myself. No longer would I wait for someone to validate me and bless me as an author. Instead I would act and be one. Screw-ups, mistakes, cluelessness and all, I would take the steps necessary to make my dream become a reality.

Each day I needed to start over and commit to myself. A workshop at the end of a book wasn't going to help me. Sure, an exercise might help me in the moment, but I needed something that would help me over years of time. I needed a surefire way to succeed so that when I fell, and fall I would, I could get back up and start over again.

Really Set a Schedule

I've been reading about the power of habits and how our minds can latch onto them. We probably have more bad habits than we want to admit. Why not create some good ones? If you've forgotten what my schedule is from the beginning parts of this book, here it is again:

Sunday: Long run
Monday: Write
Tuesday: Short run

Wednesday: Write
Thursday: Short run
    Friday: Write
    Saturday: Write

Take a piece of paper, write down your schedule, stick it where you'll see it first thing in the morning, and then do it.

But how? How to stick to the work? How many times have you started and then given up on a goal? How many of us set New Year's resolutions and actually stick to them?

When I committed to the work, I had a "come to Jesus" moment with myself. I could stay in bed and sleep or I could get up and do the work. In the beginning, it's easy. But when life gets harder, kids are sick, or you need to travel for work, then keeping up on the work isn't so easy. I remember the winter of 2010. I had taken a break from writing *Lost* because I wanted to spend time with my family for the holidays and my day job was extremely hard (when isn't it?). Taking some time off stretched out to a few weeks, and I had to make a decision. Did I really want to write the book or was it too hard and I wanted to give up?

I asked myself that question and thought about what writing meant for me. I didn't think about my family and whether they would think I had failed. No, I took a look at my life and accepted that I was going to die one day. I had reached thirty-eight years of age and either now was the time for me to embrace my dreams and go for it or I should just give up on the idea. I chose to write, finish the book, and keep trying.

What will you decide? Block out all the voices in your head. Go for a walk, find a place of calm, and really think about what you want to do. You don't need exercises at the end of this book. All you need is a desire to try to keep that flame alive.

Meditation, exercise, eating right, visualization, reading, writing, researching, and networking. Figure out how to balance the work you need to do in your life, try it, and adjust as needed. When I started training for my first marathon, I tried running four days a week and kept getting injured. I just couldn't do four days of running a week with all the other work in my life. My body needed the extra rest so I kept the schedule to three days a week. There are times when I need to skip writing, but I'm okay with that. I can either make the time up or let it go. But the writing habit has become so ingrained in me that I look forward to it. The struggle in the early months has gone away and now become a habit that is part of my normal routine.

If I go into a venture thinking that it's impossible, then, yes, I can't do it. But if I look at just today, and build upon that success, then, over time, my work builds on itself. I started out running two blocks, and over a few years, I built that up to 26.2 miles. The same is true with writing. Maybe you can write 500 words today. Build up your successes over time, and soon you'll have 80,000 words.

The secret I can share with you is that the work is hard in the beginning. When I was learning how to plot, develop characters, and make a book complete, I didn't know where to start. To overcome that challenge, I gave myself the freedom to write whatever I wanted for my first draft. Now when I sit down to write the first draft of a book, it's my favorite part of the process. Practice has helped me get into my flow a lot easier. I can sit down, envision the scene in my head, and just type what I "see" in my mind. Sometimes I struggle to keep up because the ideas are going faster than I can type.

We all need to start somewhere, and I don't know what works for you, but I do have some suggestions.

Writing the Book

My wife and I have an ongoing disagreement that's gone on now for more than a decade. When she asks me "How do you get the work done?", I tell her that I simply just put my mind to it and do the work. After I give her my answer, a round of questions come back about whether I doubt myself, don't want to do the work, or if I'm afraid of failure, and I need to be careful because my answers might come off conceited or snobby. I made a commitment to myself to write, and I honor that.

I do not have any special secret to how to write books. When I compare myself to others, I often feel inadequate because I don't understand (yet) how other authors are cranking out books so quickly. But, over time, I'm realizing there's a mind shift here. If I think I'm going to fail, then I am. To overcome the obstacles, I show up and do the work. There isn't really anything more to it than that. But my wife doesn't want to hear me say that because it comes off pompous.

Instead of talking about writing, reading about writing, or learning about writing, just write! Sit down, type or use a pen and paper, and get to work. What do I do when I see the blank screen? I make certain I have a thread to work on before I start my writing. For example, I am often daydreaming throughout the course of the day. I get my ideas while running, cleaning, and doing other physical work. When creative ideas come to me, I write them down (email them to myself or start a Google document) and then think through the plot. Sometimes my ideas come to me in the form of dreams or I'm inspired by life events. Whatever the case, I mull over the idea in advance of sitting down and writing.

When I do start working, I then imagine what that character is doing and who she is talking with and frame out a general idea of where the story will go. On a writing day, I fire up the laptop, write, and do my best to end my writing time by keeping the idea alive by leaving a thread open for me to continue. Since I'm writing on a regular basis, I'm giving myself time to think about the plot during my work commute, and the next day I can pick up where I left off. Over time, I've framed the plot of the novel and can write to that.

The challenge comes when I discover an important part of my novel while I'm writing. That's one of my favorite times to write because I'm discovering the story as I go along as will the reader. In *Lost*, I wrote the first draft and had a breakthrough after the first draft was written. I modified the book and changed it because the reveal worked and made the book stronger.

What I've learned is that if I write every day or every other day, I can hold the plot in my head and can easily pick up the narrative threads and continue writing without any problems. When I stop writing for weeks, well, let's just say that I get rusty and can't remember all the specifics about the book. I make the work harder when I don't write regularly. When I do write on a regular basis, a few things are happening. I'm not only strengthening my ability to write because I'm honing my skills, but I'm also familiarizing myself with a regular habit.

There are tools you can use to help you. If you're a hands-on type of person, then buy a box of index cards and create cards for each character. Describe the character, list their personality traits, and tack that up on a wall. Do the same thing with major locations and plot points. Each time you look at the creative board, you'll have a means of linking the plot to the characters in a way that is both visual and concrete.

If you're more of an abstract person, then use software such as Scrivener to create a similar digital environment to outline your book. When you know who the characters are, you can then start adding in the conflict and build up the plot in a way that will work to your writing style.

If you're working full-time at a day job, finding a long block of time to write might not be possible. For me, I can squeeze in forty-five minutes to an hour in the morning during the work week and then more time on Saturday morning. When I first started out writing books once I had a family, I used the early morning hours because my kids were still in bed. Later in the day I spent time with my family, did chores, and made myself present so that I wasn't an absent dad.

During a book launch, I needed to spend more time working because I had deadlines to meet and an additional amount of work to do, so I pulled back on working on a new book. While I'm working on a book, I set goals and do my best to meet them. When I wrote *Awakenings* in a month, the biggest challenge was that I had to neglect other aspects of my life, and the pressure of writing approximately 1,700 words a day (no matter what) weighed heavily on me.

Find the schedule that works for you, try it out, and adjust it as needed. Over the last few years, I started thinking about my writing careers as a business. When I go to my day job, I do so because I want to show up. I want to contribute, be part of a team, and be compensated as such. I don't think about whether my "muse" inspires me. I go to work every day and work hard.

With writing, I have taken the same approach. My second job is being an author. I haven't decided to do all this extra work because I have nothing better to do or work when I feel like it. No, I made a commitment to myself and want to keep that promise because I've invested time and energy into my writing career. I want to show up and write because it's been a lifelong dream of mine to be an author.

My books aren't going to write themselves, and I'm not going to become a better marketer on wishing and hoping. I need to put in the time and do the work. The secret is to make being an indie author fun by realizing I am finally making the time to do what I've always loved. There are tips to learn how to write a book, but the key point is to commit to doing it and then following through.

Research

Before you start your next book, what worked and what didn't from your first one? And if you haven't written a book yet, then what is the book about? Did you do the research that you wanted to do? With little time to do the actual writing, I still make time for research and collect all the information in Scrivener.

To help me in my research phases, I have even set up folders in Google Drive and then saved my work on the go. I sometimes don't know if I'm going to have some free time before work, on my train ride to and from work, or after the kids are in bed. Because I don't quite know when I'll have some dedicated time, I like having the various Google Apps on my phone so that I can do the research I need wherever I'm at without any problems. In a pinch, I've even done some work while waiting in the checkout line at the supermarket. No matter if I am writing notes or ideas to myself, I like having flexibility on when and where I can work.

For visuals, I have also created a private Pinterest board and pinned various images there to help me with locales, character designs, cover ideas, and anything else that I can think. The cool thing with Pinterest and Google Drive is that I can share access to any of the content I put there with a partner, graphic designer, or anyone else I'm working with on the project.

I really enjoy Scrivener, though it took me some time to learn how to use, but with mobile apps such as Pocket and Evernote available, there are many ways you can track your new ideas and creative brainstorm processes if you try Scrivener and it's not for you.

And as I've mentioned before, if pen and paper works for you, go for it. I like index cards that I hang up, but I can't easily bring them with me. I take photos of all my work on the index cards and save it, but seeing the photos on the small screen on my phone isn't the best. Though going down this route helps in a pinch.

Reading

When I'm starting out again and working on my next project, I often have trouble making time for reading. I read business-related articles, learn about the publishing industry, and keep up on the Facebook indie publishing groups I'm involved in, but I do have trouble making time to read for fun. I typically become swamped with trying to juggle all the various parts of writing a book, and my reading time is a few minutes right before I go to bed each night. My wife can attest that I'll read a few pages before bed and she'll see me struggling with holding up my book or Kindle. I'm lying on my back, have all intentions of reading a good amount, and then I fight with holding the book up and keeping my eyes open. The struggle is real and I jolt myself awake, push the book back up so I don't get smacked in the face, and discover I lost my spot on the page. I start again, the lids of my eyes become heavy, and then—whack—the book hits me on the nose. I roll over, put the book down, and it's lights out. Pretty sad, I know.

Like everyone else, I am pulled in many different ways. Back in the late '90s, I'd get on the morning train and see the readers holding heavy Harry Potter books and I'd smile. Over time, Kindles appeared, then faded away, and now most people are glued to their phones. I pay attention to what people are doing and see that commuters are checking email, on Facebook, playing video games, and some even watching shows on Netflix. I see very few people reading books these days. Of course, my research is unscientific, but there's a kernel of truth there: With so many options competing for people's entertainment time, a book (or ebook) is not the first choice any longer. Why read a book when you can catch up on the shows you missed last night because your kid was sick? The world has changed and people are adapting to using technology in different ways.

With juggling so many different responsibilities, I also find it challenging to make time to read. But reading is important because I need to do two things:

1. Understand the market (what's selling and why)
2. Have fun

I have a hard time with the "have fun" option. In the summertime, I tend to pick a popcorn type of book and will read whatever the latest *Star Wars* book is because I'm just looking for something that I don't have to think a lot about. And I don't want to see everything I do as work. There are times when I just want to read for pleasure.

The reason why I wanted to be a writer is to entertain by sharing my creative ideas with the world. Not making time to do that gets me off track. There are books that I have read that changed my life and made all the difference to me. Some books have surprised me with how emotionally invested I became with the characters (John Green, I'm looking at you. Your *Fault in Our Stars* blew me away.).

The challenge in being an indie author is to try to be as efficient and productive of a writer as I can. However, I can't schedule every minute of my life. I need to leave room for serendipity to grace herself in my day. Sometimes taking the unforeseen path or picking up a book that I don't know much about makes the most difference in my life because I'm inspired in ways that are raw, beautiful, and true.

Reading has always been the best and cheapest way for me to use my imagination and explore what is not possible. Shakespeare saw the works of the other playwrights of his day and pulled in other sources for his own plays. The beauty of what he did was to shine a light on the essential human personality traits, and his works remain timeless. I am working on reading more for pleasure than for "competitive research." But the struggle is real: If I have limited time to spend with family and friends, I choose to watch a TV show with my family or a movie so we share an experience. With reading books, yes, I read to my daughter when putting her to bed each night, but I also struggle to make more time to read for me. One of my current pleasure reads is Kristine Kathryn Rusch's *Diving Universe*. Now I just need to make more time to read the next book!

Chapter 14: Are You Happy?

I've shared a lot about all the hard work an indie author needs to do on a daily basis. It's hard. Really hard. I don't know any author who just writes, knocks out the words, and then sits back, stares up at the puffy clouds, and sips on a nice cup of green tea. Sure, there might be authors out there who don't have to focus on marketing, but that's not my experience with the authors I know.

Typically, we're working our full-time day job, putting in extra hours there working on a deadline, and then come home, trying to squeeze in writing in the late or wee hours of the morning (Today I started writing at 5:15 a.m., and the clock is ticking down toward my deadline because I need to take my son to school and rush off to work.).

The question that I ask myself, from time to time, is:

Am I happy?

Yes, I also ask, as I mentioned previously, "Is this healthy for me?", but I like to check in on my statement of happiness.

Am I happy? With life, work, writing, where I'm at, sure, the whole ball of wax.

In the years that I have actively been writing and publishing books, I have found there are times when I go on autopilot. I put my head down and get to work. The work then bleeds into the everyday ritual of all the other things I need to do, and without time for reflection, there is the danger of burnout.

I think there are times when I'm too narrow minded on the task in front of me, and I hunker down, struggling to complete the work. My stubbornness rises up, and I work harder instead of smarter. The cost of all the work can be devastating. Lack of sleep over months or years can affect decision making, mood, and your overall health.

Freestyle Journaling

One of my favorite ways of writing is to sit down at a computer and just start writing. In trying to come to terms with the state I'm in, simply writing "Am I happy?" at the top of the page and then writing the response can be freeing and uplifting—if you're willing to address your true feelings.

At the time that I write this, it's 5:20 a.m., and I'm trying to squeeze in some writing before I need to head out the door for work by 6:45 a.m. I have a short window to write, and then I'm off at my day job. But how do I truly feel? I'm worried and afraid that the words I write won't resonate with people, or worse, that people will ridicule or look at this book and say, "But he's not a successful writer? He's not making a lot of money. He's a failure."

And how happy am I about my current state as an author? I have sacrificed a lot to be here and believe that if I continue to work at a smart pace—giving myself time to rest and be with my family—that I will see greater success. The vision I have ahead in front of me is a long journey that's on a slight incline. There are milestones along the way and people I will meet who help me and others I will offer help.

I am happy that I am taking a risk to take the creativity inside me and allowing myself the opportunity to share that with the world. I do not want to remain silent any longer, and the act of creation for me is extremely fulfilling and freeing. To have an idea, foster it, and then shape it into a book is something I have dreamed about since I was a kid. I've since discovered that not only can I write a book, but I have found a repeatable process I am learning to hone over time.

Just within the last week, I have networked with different indie authors (Thank you Facebook groups!) and asked advice on pricing options for cover designs and proofreading. I've looked at my expenses and am looking to find ways to continue releasing quality products, but I need to do so at a lower cost. How do I do that? Where do I go? Who do I talk to?

In the past, I would have fretted over these decisions and become frustrated because I didn't know how to reach out to the right people. But over time, I'm not only learning how to come out of my introverted shell more (I was interviewed on a podcast last summer and gave a workshop about how to use social media, for Pete's sake!). The little baby steps I am making to pursue an indie author career are blossoming, slowly, yes, but there is forward movement, and I'm starting to see success in ways I could not have imagined.

That possibility for a better and more fulfilling future is making me happy. I am no longer the slave to the negative thought process of: "Oh, maybe one day I will write a book." Or, worse yet: "Maybe one day a big publishing house will choose to publish my book. I'm just going to keep trying with this one book I wrote almost thirty years ago when I was a kid." No. I am not that person any longer.

The writing I have done over the past eight years has not only taught me how to be a better writer, but I have also changed and am willing to take more risks, to work hard for what I believe in, but I now know my own limitations. I have worked extremely hard over the last eight years and can admit I have sometimes complained about the small amount of money I have made. In my head, I keep thinking of the large number of small businesses that fail each year and wonder if I'm a failure too. Am I happy? Would I be happier if I were to stop?

The tricky part of the equation is my realizing that in order to sell more books, not only do I need to become a better writer (and I'll only do that by writing more and more), but I also need to become a better marketer. I need to understand why people buy books, how to sell my books, and make that connection with my tribe—readers who will pick up my book and identify with the characters and their struggles.

That is what I have wanted for a long, long time. Readers to "get me" and say, "I can see why Cinderella did what she did because she was lonely and sad." There's a specific message of hope in my books that carries through. Often my main female protagonists have been abandoned by family and struggle to find happiness and love. They often make mistakes and stumble along the way but then discover their own path to finding the peace and love they've always searched for in their lives. The final reveal is the understanding that they needed to love themselves first and they don't need a prince (or any man) to save and rescue them.

I am most happy when I have the freedom to write what I love and know. When I come up with creative worlds and can see those play out in my head, I become one with my idea and the words just flow out on the page. The hard work that causes me to be unhappy is trying to make time to learn all the skills that I need to be successful. I enjoy learning, but there is so much change and disruption in the publishing industry that's it's been difficult to keep up.

And once I answer the question "Am I happy?", the next logical question is: Do I want to continue writing? Do I need to stop? Would I be happier if I didn't write anymore?

The hard answer that came to me back in 2015 was that, yes, I needed to regroup, change my priorities, and shift them from obsessively driving myself too hard to finish books in order to measure up with the rest of the indie publishing world. Taking some time to reflect, rest, and recharge my batteries was not easy for me. I felt like a failure seeing the strain on my marriage and kids as I desperately tried to juggle and keep all the balls in the air. I compared myself to the successful indie authors in the news and wondered, "Why can't I have success like that? What am I doing wrong? What's wrong with me?"

The truth was that I had a long way to go, and instead of beating myself up, I needed to give myself the space to fail, to feel the frustration and anger at how little time I had to work. I needed to answer hard questions that kept coming up:

Should I quit working full-time?
Where would the money come in?
What about healthcare?
Do I even want to quit my job?
Am I good enough?
What if I fail?
Why is this so hard?

Question upon question came up, and I became fixated on whether I was succeeding or not.

After I took some time to reflect, go to counseling with my wife, and lessen the pressure, I learned that I needed a healthier path to move forward. I could not do it all. I just couldn't. It wasn't healthy for me to push myself so hard and for so long. I needed a path and a plan that would be easy to follow so that I wouldn't get distracted and one that would also be flexible for when I needed to spend more time at my day job or be more present with my family.

I am most happy when there is balance in my life. Many moons ago, my English literature professor taught us about the Golden Mean or *le juste milieu*. He taught us the importance of finding balance in one's life and not going to extremes. I have carried that lecture and the lessons I learned in class that day with me for nearly thirty years. I knew a long time ago that I do not like to be pigeonholed in being a "director of web technology" or "a writer" or "marketer." I am me.

I wear many hats and hope to wear many more as I learn new skills. For many years, I wasn't a "runner," but now I'm not only that but also a "marathoner." The changes that have come to me in life have happened because of a particular moment in time. I feared turning forty and not truly following my dreams. It was that simple and cliché. I made a conscious decision to start writing again, and it's been an amazing journey so far.

You now know my story, but now it's time for you to answer: Are you happy? Be honest with yourself. You might be surprised with what you discover.

Chapter 15: In It for the Long Haul

The mindset that I've adopted is one of a marathon runner rather than a sprinter. When I first started out, I wanted to spring out of bed and win the race fast, but I became tired, frustrated, and frankly, angry. I was jealous that some writers were making a six-figure-income while I toiled away and struggled to get my first book out.

I took a long, hard look at my life and had to come to terms with my jealousy, frustration, and anger. I needed tools and habits that would help me learn a new way of working. In looking back, adding running to my weekly routine was probably one of the smartest things I could have done because the repetitive nature of running helped me not only with discipline and willpower but also gave me the space to think.

When I run, I do not run with music or any type of distraction. In the really bad parts of winter, I do run on a treadmill and I watch video podcasts, but normally, I just run outside with all of nature around me. There are a lot of fads that come and go in the indie publishing world. I've seen people flare up with great ambition and success only to fade away because they burn themselves out. I subscribe to the approach that I'm building a career. I'm not looking for a scheme to get rich quickly. I am choosing to build a relationship with my readers and want to share with them the best possible stories that I can write. I'm a storyteller and enjoy using my imagination to create new worlds and populate those realms with unique people.

I wrote my first story at nine and my first book at sixteen, and when I look back at the crazy road I traveled to get to where I am today, it's pretty amazing. The internet didn't exist when I first started writing. When I wrote the first draft of *Dorothea's Song*, I used a word processing program on my Commodore 64 computer and had to break the chapters apart because there wasn't enough memory to hold all the scenes in one file. I had 5 ¼" floppy disks with my novels, then 3 ½" disks, and now Google Drive. Today we have augmented reality and virtual reality along with Audible. Movies are in 3D and the room for expansion in having a series come to life on HBO, Amazon, or Netflix is a real possibility.

Technology will continue to change, evolve and become more integrated with what we as humans do on a day-by-day basis. My job is to adapt and be as nimble as I possibly can, understanding not just how to be the best writer I can be but also the best marketer.

Artificial Intelligence

In one year, Google changes their search algorithm 500 to 600 times. With home assistants coming into the marketing (Google Home, Alexa, Cortana, and Siri), how people discover and find entertainment and content will continually evolve. Today Google Home allows you to look up the weather, play music from Spotify, and make a reservation at a local restaurant using OpenTable. And that's today as I write this book. I can only imagine what the assistants will be able to do a year or two years from now. San Francisco is starting to have Uber driverless cars. Our world is changing faster than we can probably keep up with all the new technology. But the possibility is there for all of us to join in the excitement and fun.

Our books are not simply books. They are products that are indexed in the world's search engines. The more products we have out, that are search engine optimized by area of interest or concept, matching to what readers want, the better chance we have of being discovered.

In today's world, the Google search I make in Philadelphia will be different than the same search in Beijing, China. Results are local, and if we're tied into Google, our search history can be used to help the search engine predict what we're looking for in our search. Welcome to the world of machine learning and artificial intelligence.

When we write, I believe it to be of the utmost importance that we understand the marketing and technology around us. Knowing how digital ads work with tracking pixels and retargeting can help us create successful marketing campaigns. But if you are working full-time, how can you learn all that you need to know?

Align Your Interests and Goals

I learned back in college that I could work smart or burn myself out. I chose to be a double major and studied English literature and French. I had to read a lot of books, analyze them, and write papers. To help me, I often took a theme and wrote it up for my

English class, but then I took that same theme and used it for my French class. The papers were entirely different, but I aligned the studying and research that I needed to use to complete my assignments. I saved time by blending together what I needed to learn in each class to make my life more bearable.

I have carried that philosophy and work ethic all through my life. I taught myself how to create podcasts, and then I pitched the idea to my day job and we did podcasts. I practiced using social media and set the accounts up at my day job. I'm learning about journey mapping and SEO at my day job and am applying that knowledge to my author career. I've chosen careers that have a natural symbiotic relationship with my writing goals. I work in a marketing and communications division, and what I learn there, I can apply to my indie author career. And similarly, I started experimenting with Google Tag Manager and could intelligently discuss the implementation of that product at my day job.

Whatever career you're in, can you find a way to overlap your two worlds? If you're a plumber, can you use the knowledge you've gained on the job and incorporate your experience into your books? Maybe you're a science fiction writer and you can apply your plumbing experience in a novel about building the first water delivery systems on a burgeoning Mars colony? The possibilities are endless.

Because we have limited free time, learning how to apply our skills with that of our writing life will not only make our lives easier but speaks nicely to the "write what you know" adage that is often quoted by writers.

Whatever you can do to align your day job and your author career, I highly recommend doing so in order to help maximize your growth potential. It doesn't matter what you do for a living, there's probably a way to take some of what you do and weave that into your stories. If you happen to be in marketing or communications, then you can use your skills to help you sell your books and build your audience.

Mind, Body, and Soul

If we are lucky, we are on this Earth for decades. The time will sometimes go slowly, and other days, days will fly by faster than we might want. I am making a conscious effort to focus on how I think, taking care of my body and embracing the entwinement of my thoughts and body, expressed through my feelings. I know that if I think negatively, then the outcome is going to be negative. If I want success, I need to envision it and work toward it, and when I fail, pick myself up and try again. I need to listen, learn, and adapt to an ever-changing world around me. The work is hard, but the unknown is sometimes so overwhelming that I lose faith.

In the wee hours of the morning, I sometimes wake up from a bad dream and fall back on my pillow, taking in all that I have to do and how long the road is ahead of me. Recently, I had a dream in which I received an envelope in the mail and I was so happy. The envelope contained a large sum of money from my author earnings. I took the large bill out and showed it to my wife. A wave of pride washed over me, and when I showed it to her, the bill changed to be a much smaller amount.

I woke up the next morning and thought about that dream. The fear that I have within me that I'm "not good enough" and that I cannot earn enough money to support my family on my writing is a real concern. I'm sharing this with you because I think it's important that I be transparent and honest on where I am in the journey, showing where I've failed but also how far I've come. Writing hasn't been easy, and I would tell others if they're not really enjoying the work, then they might want to consider another career. Success does not come overnight. (Sure, it might seem that way for some, but those rare occurrences are a flash in the pan. The majority of indie authors struggle to make a living off their books.)

I believe that if we want to earn more, be discovered by more readers, and have greater success, then we need to understand how readers are buying books. Or, how they're not. Maybe readers use the library or Kindle Unlimited, read the book once without ever owning it, and move on to the next book in the series. And if they can't find the book in Kindle Unlimited or a library, then they find the next writer.

While I have worked on writing books, learning marketing, and putting my hard effort into my full-time day job, I've not had much time left for other parts of my life. The constant push and pull of deadlines and responsibilities is an ever-evolving challenge.

Over the last few years, I've read book after book that promises to teach me the secrets of how to be successful in indie publishing, but I've not seen a book that focuses on the delicate balance between taking care of yourself and building your author career. The skills that I have learned over the past eight years have taken me on a journey, and when I look back to where I was to where I am now, I am amazed. I hope that this book has inspired you to finish your first book or start your twentieth. When I am finished, I'll reflect and then move on to my own next project (yes, Cinderella, I hear you calling my name). Little by little, I'll add what I've learned and apply it to my daily routine.

Tomorrow and Tomorrow and Tomorrow

The work ahead is immense. And for me to achieve my goals, I need to chunk out the work into bite-sized pieces, but that's also true of working on my own personality quirks and flaws. I use meditation to reflect on myself to ensure that I am not short-changing my family and those I love with any pent-up anger and frustration due to juggling two careers at once. I think that the logical question that you might ask is: Then why do you still have a full-time job? Why not just quit it and write?

In all honesty, my answer is twofold: I do love my job because I work with amazing people and the projects that I work on are making a difference in the world. The work I do at my day job is also giving me an opportunity to learn, and that symbiotic relationship between what I do at my job and in writing is integral to me. I use the one to feed the other. But if I'm honest with myself, I'll admit that I'm also afraid. Quitting and putting all my eggs in one basket is a grand gesture that I'm not comfortable with at this period in my life. I like working full-time at my day job. It's nice having sick days, a retirement plan, vacation, and a steady income. Good things to have when raising kids.

When Amazon switched their algorithms and then added Kindle Unlimited, authors who had been earning well saw a tremendous drop in their incomes. Without recourse, they had to drop out and find new ways to earn money because they were not prepared for the change that took place. I enjoy writing, but I also would like to have the stability of a paycheck and benefits for my family. Maybe you're in the same point in your life, and that's okay. I understand that. I do still feel the tweak of frustration that I don't have the time to spend eight hours a day writing, researching, and learning marketing for my books.

I could be negative or look at the long road ahead of me. Today I sat down and did some writing. In fact, I finished this book. That's a good thing. Tomorrow I will do other work and the tomorrow after that I'll take what I've done and build a future for myself by investing in learning new skills and applying them to my next book. The successes do build up over time. Not everything will happen overnight, and I would much rather have a solid foundation through which I can build a future than to toss the dice at a get-rich-quick scheme. The fads come and go, but I want to be around for the long term, and in order to do that, I need to be mindful of where I am today and find peace with that.

I hope this book has been of help to you. I know that it's been helpful to me because I've now put down all that I've learned over the years, and I'm happy to see that. And what's refreshing is that I'm also seeing the road ahead. Yes, I have a long way yet to go, but the journey is inviting and can be fun—if I allow it to be. Be good to yourself, take stock of where you are, and I wish you the best in your author career. How many people get a chance to not only find their passion in life but then actually do it? I wish you the best in your writing. Let me know how you're doing on your journey. And most of all, please, take care of yourself, and I hope you enjoy the wild and twisted journey of living the life of an indie author!

Appendix

I compiled the major takeaway points from this book to help remind you what can help you on your author career. Remember, I focus on the mind, body, and soul. Each area here is meant to be integrated with another section, forming a life plan to help you succeed.

Schedule

Sunday: Exercise
Monday: Write
Tuesday: Exercise
Wednesday: Write
Thursday: Exercise
Friday: Write
Saturday: Write

Practical Help to Lower Stress

Close your eyes, and take a deep breath while slowly clenching your left fist. Keep your left fist clenched tight for a few seconds and then as you exhale (slowly), release your fist. Take four seconds or so breathing in, hold two or three seconds, then exhale slowly out of your mouth while unclenching your fist. When finished, do it again.

Repeat the process with your right fist, then do the same with your left toes, right toes, clench your teeth, squeeze your eyes shut, shrug and hold your shoulders, and finally your pelvic floor muscle (Kegel). For each part of your body, clench or tighten the muscles while inhaling slowly, hold for a few seconds, and then release your muscles (unclench your toes or fist) and exhale

I found the above exercise to not only be a fantastic stress reliever, but also a way to recharge my batteries. It's a great way for me to soothe me and relax.

Light Visualization Exercise

If I have a few more minutes, I perform the following visualization technique. I lie on my back, relax and slowly breathe in through my nose. While breathing in, I imagine a warm light entering me, permeating its way through my cells, in my blood, and through my nerves, muscles, and bones. The light cleanses as it passes through me. After a few seconds, I then exhale all the darkness, hate and stress within me. I imagine impurities streaming out of my mouth as I exhale.

I then imagine the light traveling down through my body per breath. I breathe in a few seconds and the light goes all through my head, out my mouth, ears, and eyes, then down my throat, and through my shoulders, and I hold it there. On exhaling, all the fear and darkness within me is slowly expunged from my body. When I take my next breath, the light continues on past my shoulders, around and through my heart, and into my lungs, filling me with goodness and light. I continue doing this until the light has completed its journey all through my body and down through my toes.

Creative Board

Index cards for every character
Card for every location
Major plot point
Pin up all the cards on a wall, and use the cards to help inspire you as well as solve plot problems or to visualize relationships between characters, events, or locations.

Writing Tips

Plot out scenes in your head when commuting, exercising, or cleaning.
Have a word count goal for each time you write.
Track all the words your write to show progress and motivate you (smarturl.it/u56ei0)
Tell your friends and family your goal to make yourself accountable.
When you're finishing your writing for the day, leave narrative threads open so that you can more easily pick up the story the next time you write.

Networking

Join online forums
Kboards.com
Facebook groups
Heather Hildenbrand's Fiction Author Coach (FREE)
Authorpreneur Circle
20BooksTo50K
Follow authors on Twitter.

Read

Books you love, different genres, nonfiction and fiction.

Research/Learn

Listen to podcasts
The Art of Paid Traffic with Rick Mulready
(rickmulready.com/category/aoptpodcast/)
The Author Biz (theauthorbiz.com/category/podcasts/)
The Creative Penn podcast
(www.thecreativepenn.com/podcasts/)
Kobo Writing Life podcast
(kobowritinglife.com/category/kwl-podcast/)
The Rocking Self-Publishing podcast
(rockingselfpublishing.com/)
The Self-Publishing podcast
(selfpublishingpodcast.com/podcasts/)
The Smart Passive Income podcast
(www.smartpassiveincome.com/podcasts/)
Story Grid podcast (storygrid.simplecast.fm/)
The Tim Ferriss Show (fourhourworkweek.com/podcast/)
Unemployable with Brian Clark
(rainmaker.fm/series/unemployable/)
Take webinars
Read authors' blog posts
Writer Beware (accrispin.blogspot.com/)
Kristine Kathryn Rusch's Business Musing
(kriswrites.com/15371-2/)
The Creative Penn (www.thecreativepenn.com/blog)
Sign up for marketing/business online classes

Take Stock

Is this healthy for me?
Am I happy?

I hope this book has been helpful for you. If you're new and just starting out, be easy on yourself. There's a lot to learn, and an author's journey is a long one. Remember, you're not alone. Good luck!

ABOUT THE AUTHOR

Ron Vitale is a fantasy and science fiction author. He has a Master's degree in English Literature from Villanova University where he studied the works of Alice Walker and Margaret Atwood, interpreting their novels with a psychological Jungian approach by showing how the central female protagonists in their novels use storytelling as a means to heal themselves from trauma. He lives in a small town outside of Philadelphia, Pennsylvania.

In the fall of 2008, he published his fantasy novel *Dorothea's Song* as an audiobook on Podiobooks and for sale in the Amazon.com Kindle store, and in 2011 he published *Lost*, the first book in the Cinderella's Secret Diaries series, in 2012 the second book in the series, *Stolen*, was published and in 2014 the third book in the series, *Found* was released.

Ron has since published *Awakenings* and *Betrayals*, books 1 and 2, of *The Witch's Coven* series as well as *Faith*, the first book in the *Jovian Gate Chronicles*. He keeps himself busy by writing his blog, and on learning how to be a good father to his kids all while working on his next book.

Learn more at www.ronvitale.com